1.

COLOR SECTION

Sixteen color plates showing one hundred and twelve original designs by the author.

Plate I *overleaf*
Necklace crafted entirely of eighteen carat gold wire.
Constructed. Wada, 1968. Directions for constructing this necklace appear on page 113.

CONTENTS APPEAR ON PAGE 37

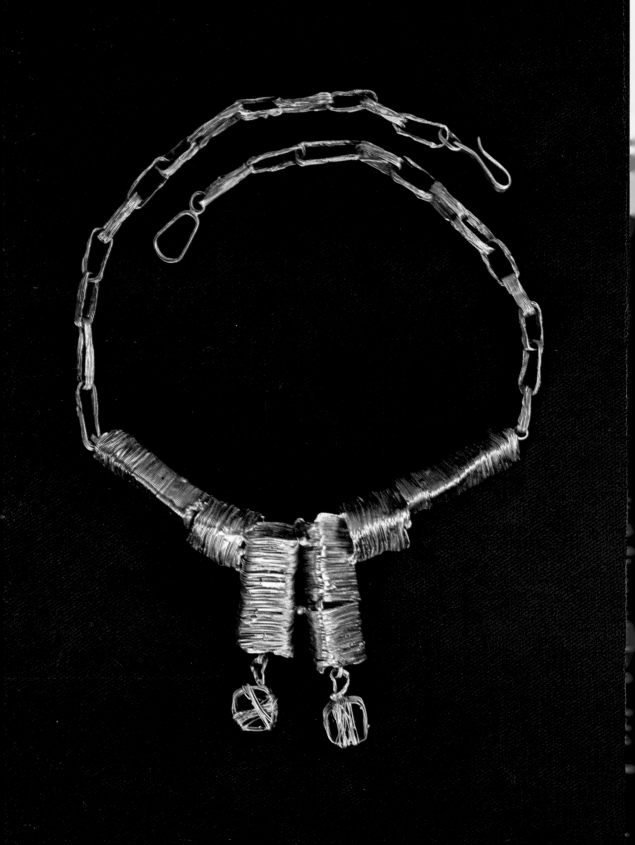

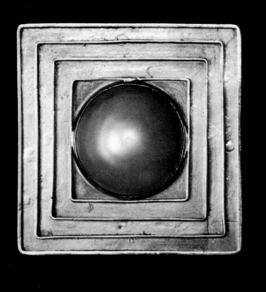

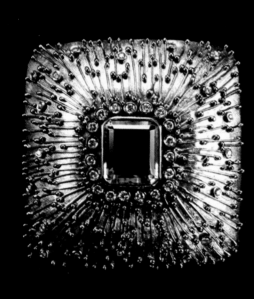
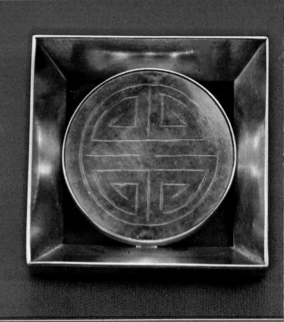

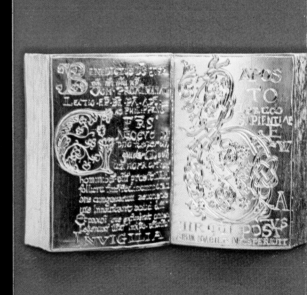

Plate II *preceding page*
RECTANGULAR PINS

Across, left to right
1. Gold plated silver brooch set with synthetic mother of pearl. Constructed. Wada, 1968.

2. Silver with crystal and green tourmaline. Constructed. Wada, 1969.

3. White gold with aquamarine and diamonds. Constructed. Wada, 1968.

4. Gold-plated silver with Oriental gem jade. Constructed. Wada, 1968.

5. Gold-plated silver with turquoise. Cast and constructed. Wada, 1968.

6. Carved gold-plated silver. Constructed. Wada, 1967.

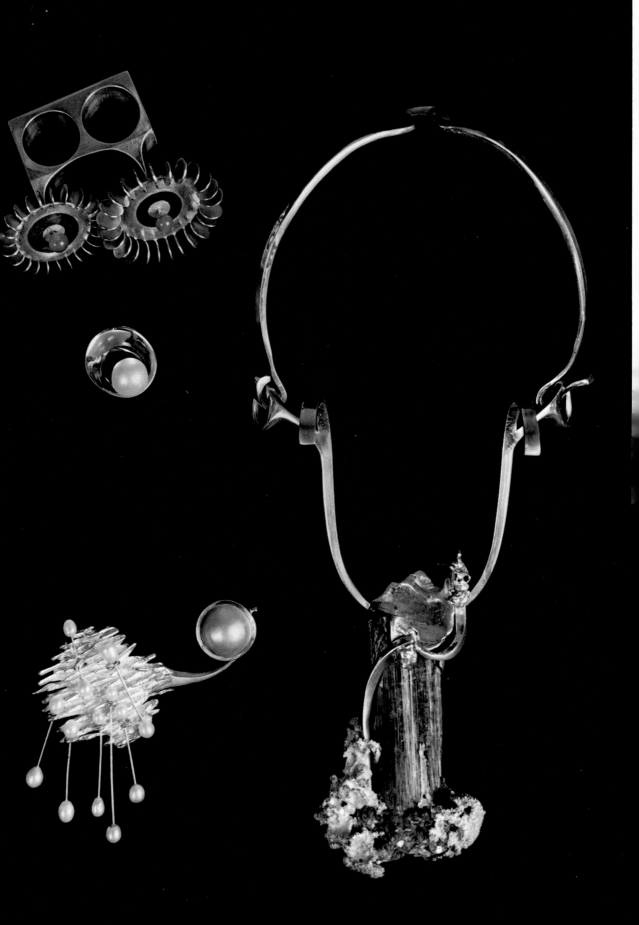

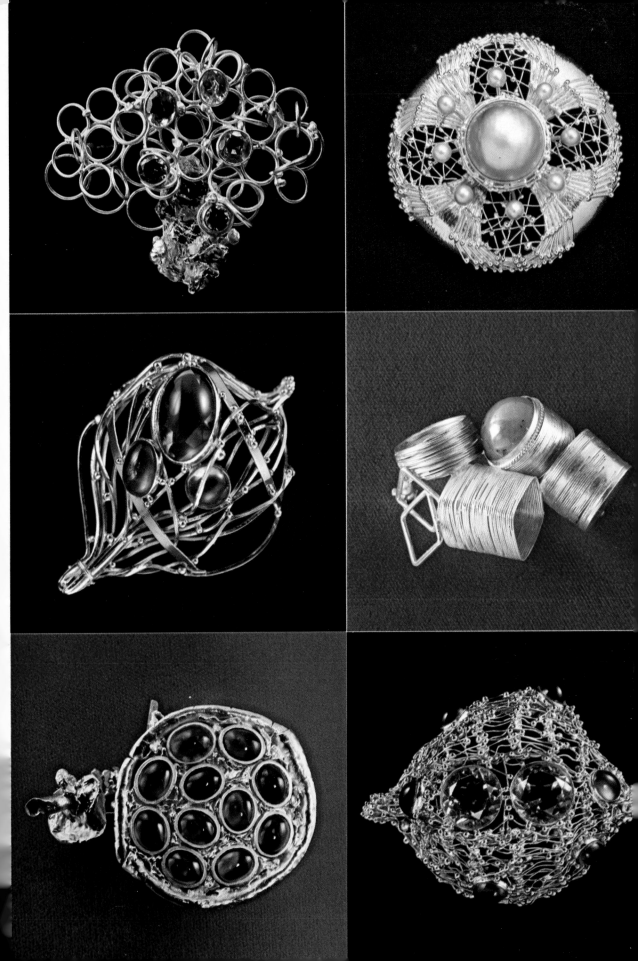

Plate IV *preceding page*
ROUND PINS

Across, left to right
1. Eighteen carat green gold with natural
aquamarine, pink tourmaline, and blue zircon.
Constructed. Wada, 1968.

2. Platinum-plated silver with mother of pearl and
pearls. Constructed. Wada, 1968.

3. Platinum-plated silver with amethyst.
Constructed. Wada, 1963.

4. Eighteen carat green gold with Chinese jade.
Constructed. Wada, 1968.

5. Fourteen carat yellow gold with garnets.
Constructed. Wada, 1965.

6. Platinum-plated silver with amethysts.
Constructed. Wada, 1965.

Plate V *overleaf*
EIGHTEEN CARAT GREEN GOLD PINS WITH TOPAZ

Top
Bow pin with topaz. Cast and constructed.
Wada, 1968.

Flare pin with yellow topaz. Constructed.
Wada, 1968.

Round pin with smoky quartz. Constructed.
Wada, 1965.

Bottom
Square shape with octagonal topaz. Constructed.
Wada, 1968.

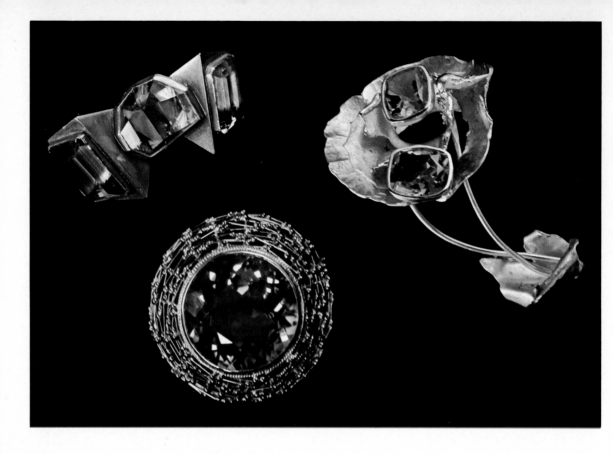

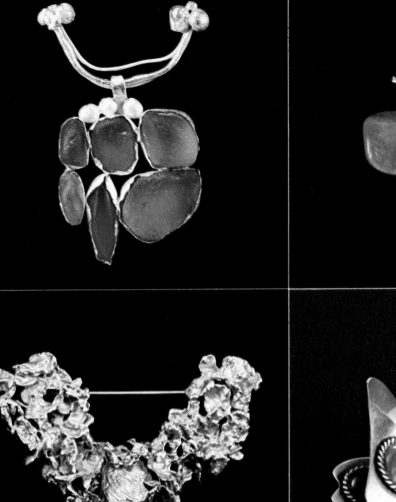

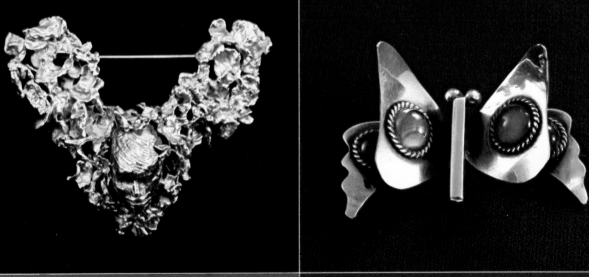

Plate VI *preceding page*
ANIMAL THEMES

Across, left to right
1. Silver pin with beach glass (bat). Constructed. Wada, 1965.

2. Silver pin with rhonite and onyx (human face).

3. Fourteen carat gold pin (golden bat). Cast and constructed. Wada, 1967.

4. Silver pin with agate (butterfly). Constructed. Wada, 1964. Instructions for making this pin appear on pages 118, 119.

5. Gold-plated silver pin with synthetic rubies and agate (cicada). Constructed. Wada, 1963.

6. Silver pin with amethyst (mice). Constructed. Wada, 1965.

Plate VII *overleaf*
GROUP OF BROOCHES

Across, left to right
1. Silver pin with flush opal. Constructed. Wada, 1964.

2. Eighteen carat gold with turquoise. Cast and constructed. Wada, 1964.

3. Platinum-plated silver with kunzite. Cast and constructed. Wada, 1967.

4. Fourteen carat white gold with aquamarine. Constructed. Wada, 1964.

5. Gold-plated silver with turquoise. Cast and constructed. Wada, 1965.

6. Silver pin with smoky quartz, blue glass, crystals, and synthetic ruby. Constructed. Wada, 1965.

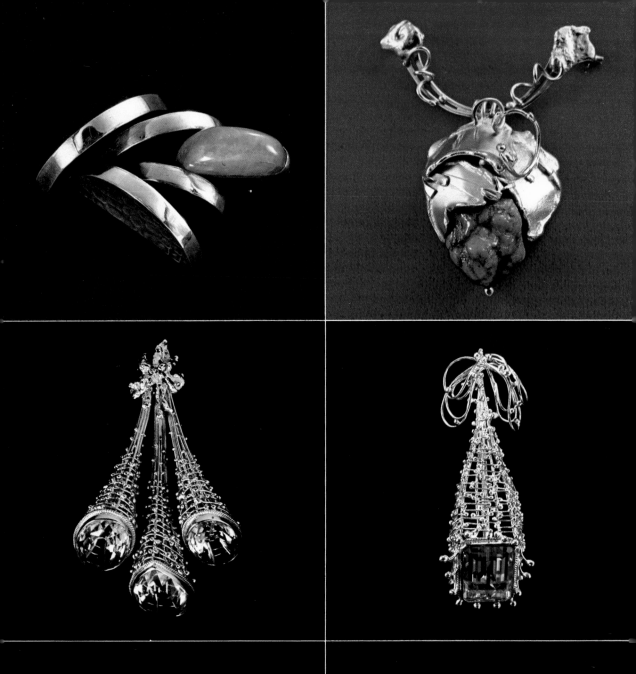

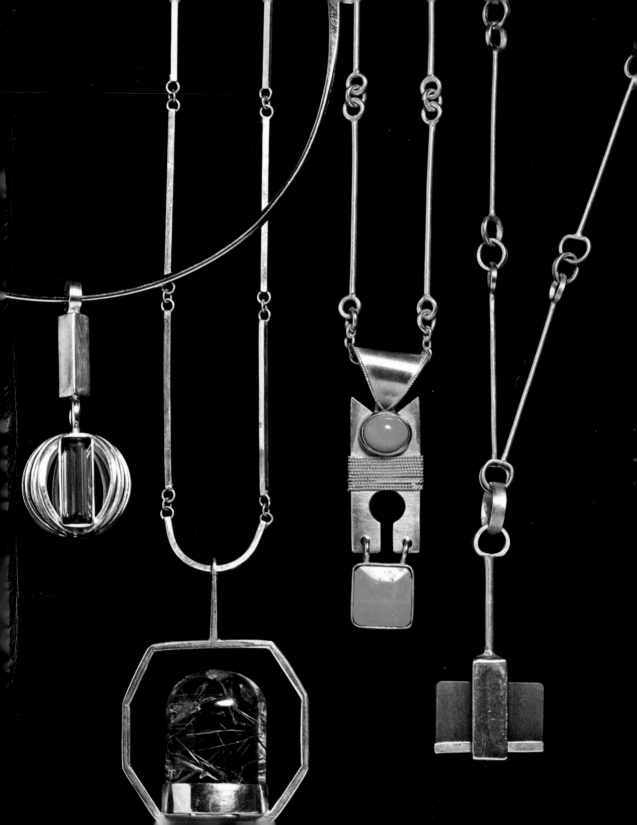

Plate VIII *preceding page*
FOUR SILVER PENDANTS

Left to right
1. Silver with synthetic amethyst. Constructed.
Wada, 1964.

2. Silver with quartz. Constructed. Wada, 1964.

3. Gold-plated silver with turquoise. Constructed.
Wada, 1964.

4. Gold-plated silver with aventurine. Constructed.
Wada, 1964.

Plate IX *overleaf*
MARINE THEMES

At left
1. Gold-plated silver pin with soladite. Constructed. Wada, 1965.

2. Gold-plated silver pin. Wada, 1964.

Center
3. Silver pin with onyx and crystal. Constructed. Wada, 1964.

4. Gold-plated silver pendant with garnets. Constructed. Wada, 1963.

At right
5. Gold-plated silver pin with turquoise. Constructed. Wada, 1962.

6. Silver pin with Philippine pearl. Constructed. Wada, 1963.

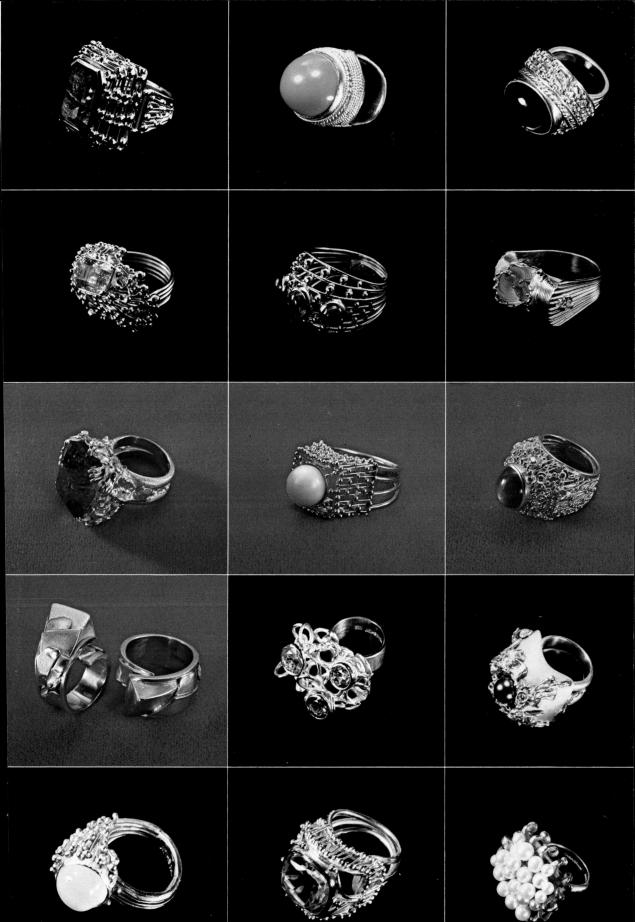

Plate X *preceding page*
GOLD RINGS

Across, left to right
1. Eighteen carat gold with pink tourmaline.
Constructed. Wada, 1968.

2. Fourteen and eighteen carat gold with turquoise.
Cast and constructed. Wada, 1960.

3. Eighteen carat gold with black star sapphire.
Constructed. Wada, 1965.

4. Eighteen and twenty carat green gold with pink
tourmaline. Constructed. Wada, 1967.

5. Eighteen carat green gold with emeralds.
Constructed. Wada, 1965.

6. Eighteen carat gold with pink tourmaline.
Constructed. Wada, 1966.

7. Eighteen carat gold with topaz. Cast and
constructed. Wada, 1968.

8. Eighteen and twenty carat yellow gold with pink
coral. Constructed. Wada, 1967.

9. Eighteen carat green gold with star sapphire and
diamonds. Constructed. Wada, 1967.

10. Fourteen and eighteen carat yellow gold with
twenty and twenty-four carat green gold.
Constructed. Wada, 1967.

11. Eighteen carat yellow gold with pink tourmaline,
blue zircon, and kunzite. Constructed. Wada, 1968.

12. Eighteen carat green gold with black pearl and
diamonds. Cast and constructed.

13. Eighteen carat gold with moonstone.
Constructed. Wada, 1968.

14. Eighteen carat yellow gold with topaz.
Constructed. Wada, 1967.

15. Fourteen carat yellow gold with pearls. Cast and
constructed. Wada, 1962.

Plate XI *overleaf*
GOLD RINGS

Across, left to right
1. Fourteen carat yellow gold. Cast. Wada, 1969.

2. Twenty and twenty-four carat gold with emerald. Constructed. Wada, 1966.

3. Fourteen and twenty carat gold with eighteen carat green gold. Cast and constructed. Wada, 1969.

4. Fourteen and eighteen carat gold with opal. Constructed. Wada, 1967.

5. Eighteen carat gold with topaz. Constructed. Wada, 1968.

6. Eighteen carat gold with opal doublet. Cast. Wada, 1967.

7. Fourteen and eighteen carat yellow gold with diamonds and sapphire. Wada, 1969.

8. Eighteen carat gold with blue sapphire and diamonds. Wada, 1968.

9. Eighteen and twenty carat gold. Constructed. Wada, 1968.

10. Fourteen carat yellow and white gold with diamonds. Constructed. Wada, 1964.

11. Eighteen carat gold with ceramic. Constructed. Wada, 1969.

12. Fourteen and eighteen carat yellow gold with opal. Constructed. Wada, 1962.

13. Fourteen and eighteen carat yellow gold with antique Roman glass. Constructed. Wada, 1964.

14. Fourteen carat yellow gold ring. Cast. Wada, 1968.

15. Fourteen and twenty carat yellow gold. Constructed. Wada, 1965.

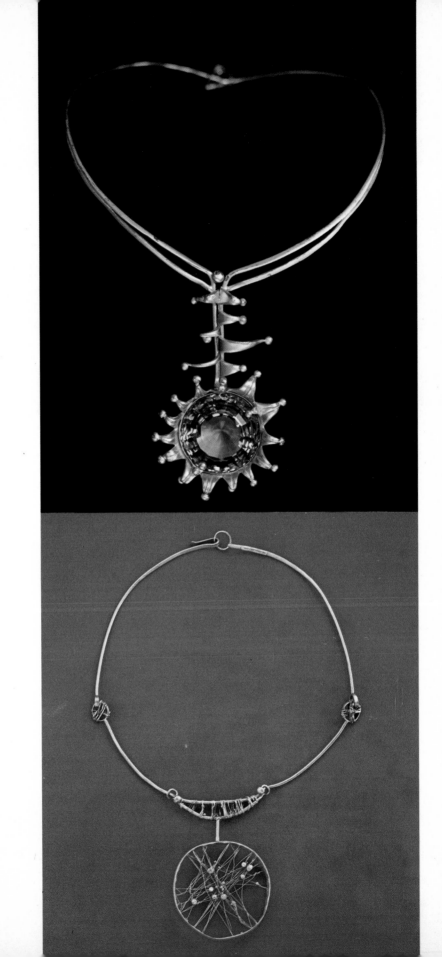

Plate XII *preceding page*
PENDANTS

Top
Gold-plated silver. Cast, forged, and constructed.
Wada, 1965.

Bottom
Fourteen and eighteen carat yellow gold.
Constructed. Wada, 1967.

Plate XIII *overleaf*
RINGS, NECKPIECES, AND PINS

Clockwise, from top left
1. Sterling silver neckpiece. Cast, forged and constructed. *Shakudo* technique. Wada, 1972.

2. Man's ring of fourteen carat cast gold. Wada, 1974.

3. Double ring, sterling silver and fourteen carat gold. Cast. Wada, 1970.

4. Choker necklace with pendant. Sterling silver and lapis lazuli. Cast and constructed. (Courtesy collection Mrs. Yoshiko Masui.) Wada, 1973.

5. Double ring, fourteen and eighteen carat gold. Cast and constructed. (Courtesy collection Mrs. Sadako Calcagno.) Wada, 1974.

6. Choker necklace with pendant. Sterling silver, fourteen and eighteen carat gold. Cast, forged, and constructed. Wada, 1973.

7. Sterling silver belt buckle with gold-plated pattern. Cast and constructed. Wada, 1974.

8. Sterling silver ring. Cast and constructed. *Shakudo* technique. Wada, 1972.

9. Sterling silver ring. Cast and constructed. *Shakudo* technique. (Courtesy collection Miss Masako Miyahara.) Wada, 1972.

10. Pin, sterling silver and fourteen carat gold. Constructed. (Courtesy collection Mrs. Kimiyo Uehara.) Wada, 1974.

Center
11. Pendant, fourteen carat gold with lapis lazuli. Cast, forged, and constructed. (Courtesy collection the Amulets and Talismans Gallery, New York City.) Wada, 1974.

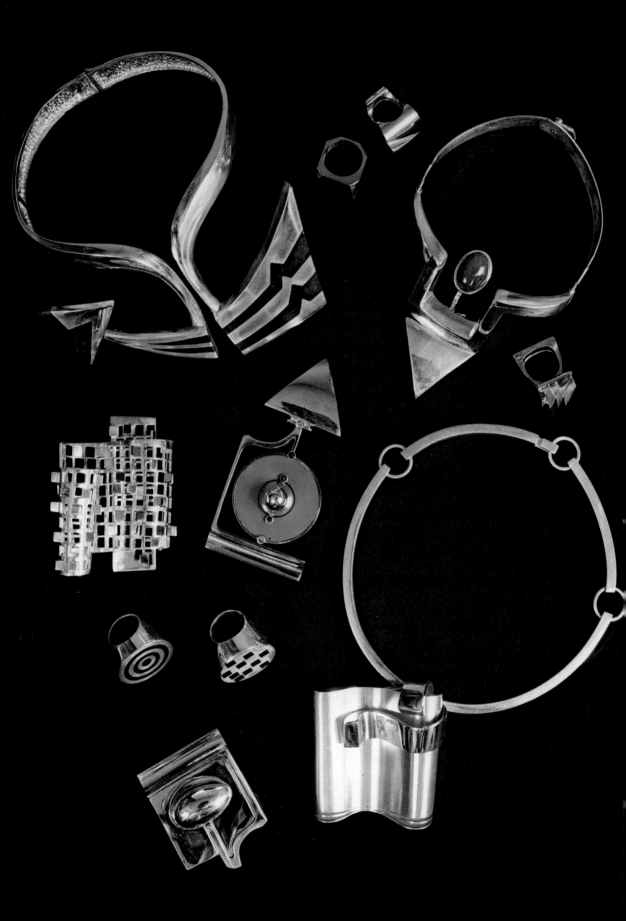

Plate XIV *preceding page*
NECKLACES AND A BRACELET

Top
Platinum-plated silver necklace with onyx, and
matching bracelet. Forged and constructed. Wada,
1967.

Bottom
Fourteen carat gold necklace with green plastic
globe. Embedded in the globe, an exotic worm from
the Amazon creates an unusual pattern. Forged and
constructed. Wada, 1967.

Plate XV *overleaf*

A BIB NECKLACE AND A HAIR ORNAMENT

Top
Platinum-plated silver necklace with pearls. Cast and constructed. Wada, 1966.

Bottom
Gold-plated silver hair ornament with synthetic zircons. Constructed. Wada, 1965.

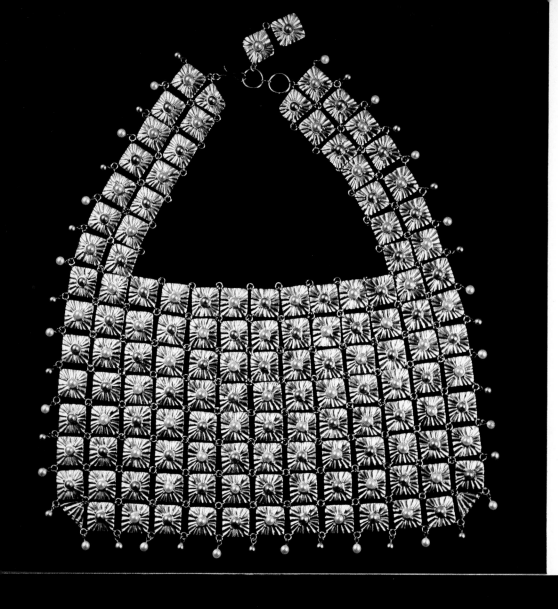

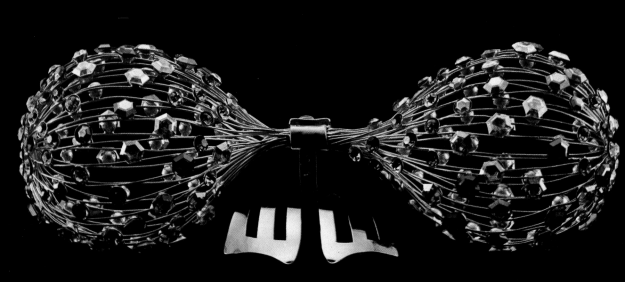

Plate XVI *preceding page*
ACCESSORIES FOR MEN

Across, left to right
1. Twelve-carat gold and silver ring. Cast and constructed. Wada, 1964.

2. Silver cuff links. Cast. Wada, 1965.

3. Fourteen-carat gold cuff links. Cast. Wada, 1966.

4. Eighteen-carat yellow gold cuff links. Constructed. Wada, 1967.

5. Silver cuff links. Cast. Wada, 1965.

6. Eighteen-carat gold cuff links with pearls. Constructed. Wada, 1965.

7. Fourteen-carat gold little finger ring with golden quartz and green tourmaline. Cast and constructed. Wada, 1967.

8. Fourteen-carat gold cuff links with opal doublet. Constructed. Wada, 1968.

9. Silver cuff links. Cast. Wada, 1966.

10. Silver ring with yellow quartz. Constructed. 1966.

11. Platinum-plated silver cuff links. Cast and constructed. Wada, 1964.

12. Fourteen and eighteen carat gold tie pin. Constructed. Wada, 1968.

13. Silver ring with onyx. Constructed. Wada, 1960.

14. Silver ring partly oxidized (black color). Cast. Wada, 1964.

The Art of
MAKING JEWELRY

The Art of
MAKING
JEWELRY

Takashi Wada

VAN NOSTRAND REINHOLD COMPANY
New York Cincinnati London Toronto Melbourne

On the jacket
Front and back jacket illustrations were designed and photographed by
Malcolm Varon in New York. They also appear with descriptive captions
as Plates III and XIII in the color section of the book.

Original Japanese edition *Tetzukuri No
Jewelry* © copyright 1968 by Takashi Wada, Tokyo.
Translated by Allan Gewirtzman.
Edited by Margaret Holton.
Color captions translated by Mr. Vasuo Uehara.

Van Nostrand Reinhold Company Regional Offices:
New York Cincinnati Chicago Millbrae Dallas
Van Nostrand Reinhold Company International Offices:
London Toronto Melbourne

Published by Van Nostrand Reinhold Company
A Division of Litton Educational Publishing, Inc.
450 West 33rd Street, New York, N.Y. 10001

16 15 14 13 12 11 10 9 8 7 6 5 4 3 2 1

Library of Congress Cataloging in Publication Data

Wada, Takashi, 1938-
  The art of making jewelry.

  Translation of Tetzukuri jueri.
  Includes index.
  1. Jewelry making — Amateurs' manuals. I. Title.
TT212.W3213 739.27 73-16715
ISBN 0-442-29149-3

CONTENTS

FOREWORD

My love affair with the art of handcrafting fine jewelry first began during my student days at the University of Art in Tokyo, where I specialized in metallurgy. Almost from the start, at every opportunity I would slip away from the supervisory eyes of my professors in order to work on my jewelry. Even when there were pressing class assignments, which I had to produce quickly, I was irresistibly impelled to spend time on my true love — making jewelry by hand. I became a captive of the art then, and my joy in it has never diminished, it has increased.

Jewelry making is pleasant work, both useful and esthetically satisfying. If you feel attracted to the craft, you will soon find yourself joyously involved. Of course, as with any worthwhile endeavor, the more you become involved the more difficult and complex the techniques become. As I work I try to devise ways to overcome problems that come up during the execution of an idea. My aim is always to create beautiful pieces of jewelry that people will admire and cherish.

In ancient times gems were valued chiefly as wealth, or as curios, and this idea persists to some degree to this day. Gems are extremely beautiful objects in themselves, of course, but their special character is revealed only when they are worn as adornments that reflect the wearer's personality.

The intrinsic value of a piece of jewelry is determined by the quality of the gem used, the metal, and the excellence of the work of the designer. Do not be dismayed if occasionally the form you realize with your hands is not true to the concept you have in your head, and you feel you have produced a disappointing piece. Always remember this: technique will improve with time and practice, but we must guard against excessive reliance on technique at the expense of experimentation. What we wish to accomplish is quality work rich in originality.

Takashi Wada

2.

PRELIMINARIES TO THE ART OF MAKING JEWELRY

GETTING STARTED

Interest in making handcrafted jewelry has increased surprisingly during the past four or five years. The thrill in the making of a piece of jewelry is in knowing you have created something beautiful, something unique, something that is yours and yours alone, from the first inspiration to the final polishing and burnishing, all done with your own heart and hands.

With the flood of mass-produced articles rising each day, the love one feels for a work one has made with great care and attention will become as deep as a treasured memory that cannot be expressed in words.

When we look at a work of art — a painting or a sculpture — usually we can envision the process that produced it. But when it comes to making a piece of jewelry by hand, people seem baffled. I am often asked to explain how it is done. They look at a piece and say, "I see. You take metal, bend it, stretch it, pare it, make holes in it . . . but . . . ," and then they are lost. Yet getting started in this craft is not as difficult as people seem to think. A young woman who had just finished her first ring told me that she had taken to jewelry making so quickly that she regretted having spent so much time trying other crafts.

Another young woman, who has been working with metal for about four years, still prizes her own works so much that, when she goes on a trip, she gathers her works together and tells her family that if something should happen to her home all she wants salvaged for herself are

the pieces of jewelry she created! This may seem a rare case, but it does demonstrate the spell that jewelry made by one's own hands can possess.

The old saying that goes, "To like something is to be skillful at it," applies to jewelry making. Recently, as the number of those who like jewelry making has grown, many of them have become sufficiently skilled to qualify as professionals. There are even some gifted students who, after studying for only a year or two, are receiving orders for custom-made pieces. But, as I noted earlier, the more progress you make, the more difficult the projects you undertake will become. You may not find this a problem while you are enjoying yourself creating personal pieces; should you decide to become a professional, however, you must face the responsibility this commitment entails.

The well-known English jewelry designer Andrew Grimm said that jewelry may be defined in three ways. First, as something in which great value is placed on the stone itself, as a piece of property; second, as a beautifully crafted object designed for its stone, a concentration of special handiwork culminating in a truly unique creation; and third, as a work of art, like that of an artist or sculptor, designed, produced, and worthy of exhibition. Your aim should be to create pieces that meet the second and third criteria. Strive for works of character, abounding in individual ideas, skilled in technique, and soaring in imagination. Consider your design carefully from every angle before you attempt to carry it out.

THE NATURE OF METALS

Silver

Pure silver is called new or white silver. Pure silver is too soft to use, so it is ordinarily mixed with copper, which may make up 5%, 7%, or 10% of the workable metal. Ordinarily, the 5% copper alloy is suitable.

When ordering silver wire, you should specify the thickness (gauge), shape (round or square), and length desired. The following thicknesses (gauges) are used fairly often for brooches, rings, and so forth.

2.0 millimeter round or square wire
1.2 millimeter round or square wire
1.0 millimeter round or square wire
0.8 millimeter round or square wire
0.4 millimeter round or square wire

Silver sheets are also used. When purchasing specify thickness (gauge), length, and width.

Gold

As in the case of pure silver, pure gold is not used as is. A gold alloy is made by combining it with silver and copper. This alloy is called carat gold. By carat we mean the proportion of pure gold in the alloy. Pure gold is rated at 24 carats (24k). In 18k gold, six parts of other metal has been added to 18 parts of pure gold. This is 75% pure gold (18/24). 20k and 18k gold are most used by designers of jewelry.

Carats	per cent of gold
24	100 (24/24)
22	91.7 (22/24)
20	83.5 (20/24)
18	75.0 (18/24)
14	58.0 (14/24)

Platinum

The Pm or Pt mark inside a ring stands for platinum. This is a metal that has a high melting point. It is also high-priced and is used with high-priced gems. White in color, it is particularly well suited for use with diamonds. Like gold, true pure platinum is soft and difficult to work. When mixed with an alloy of 10% palladium and 90% pure white gold, however, it becomes hard enough to work with.

2-1. Gauge. Device used to measure sheet metal.

White Gold

White gold is much cheaper than platinum. It is an alloy composed of nickel and pure gold. Palladium is now being added to the alloy to produce an easily workable softness. Nickel is much lighter than platinum, weighing about half as much.

Copper

Copper is one of the first metals man put to use. According to historical records, it was used by the Babylonians and Egyptians as early as 4500 B.C. and it is still highly regarded today. There is an indescribable warmth to industrial art and handmade jewelry fashioned from copper. Along with silver, copper is a good conductor of heat. One problem with copper is that it tarnishes easily, so it is a good idea to spray lacquer on a finished piece to prevent a patina from forming.

Iron and Aluminum

Although not counted among the precious metals, iron and aluminum nevertheless have interesting possibilities as media to express your ideas. They may even be best suited for your skills. Both American and European craftsmen like these metals and work with them to create fine effective pieces.

Interesting effects can also be achieved by combining metals having different characteristics, e.g., by variously fusing iron, gold, and silver. I recently tried combining rusty iron and gold. The contrast between the rough feeling of the rusted iron and the harmony of the gold produced an interesting look. Depending on how they are used, even rusty nails may be an intriguing material. In working with aluminum, colorful tinting is a possibility. It may be used to good effect in gold rings, for example, since it is so light in weight that pieces may be fairly large. Another possibility for aluminum is to join it to plastic, or to other metals.

Filings

In jewelry making, metal filings and small cuttings are produced. Do not throw these away. Have a saucer or some other receptacle at hand to collect the particles as they fall. These can be melted down again to make wire or sheeting. (You may take them to a metal dealer and have this done for you.) Be sure to keep separate the filings of the various metals such as platinum, gold, white gold, and others.

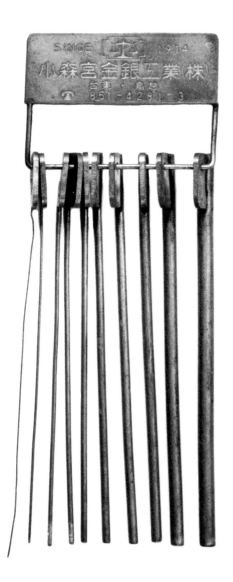

2-2. Some wire sizes.

THE NATURE OF GEMS

Ideals of beauty change with time, yet the radiant beauty of gems has remained constant throughout the ages. When I look at a gem I cannot help feeling that gems are nature's greatest works of art. It is as though the brilliance of the diamond, the ruby, and the emerald, the very wonder of the natural stone, creates in men at once a feeling of security and a sense of being lost. Such is the mysterious power possessed by gems.

From ancient times on, the value of gems has been determined by their beauty, scarcity, hardness, durability, size, quality, and the shape of the cut. While I would like to go into a detailed discussion of gems at this point, it would be better to first familiarize you with the names of major stones and some of their qualities.

In addition to such well-known gems as diamonds, emeralds, and rubies, there are other valuable stones, among them the cat's eye, star ruby, star sapphire, and alexandrite.

Tradition has it that good fortune will result from wearing the stone of the month of one's birth. Birthstones are listed below.

Platinum, gold, white gold, silver, and other metals are used to set stones. The choice of a gem depends on several factors: the color desired, the color of the skin of the person who will wear it, whether the piece of jewelry is to have a formal or an informal feeling. The metal you choose can be worked differently to produce the effect you desire. The natural shine of gold may be enhanced, or it may be given a dulled, or matte, surface. Some pieces may be oxidized (blackened) in parts and yet make use of gold, platinum, and gems.

In choosing a gem that you yourself will wear you must first of all ask yourself whether you will enjoy wearing it, and will not tire of it. Be careful when you buy. Instead of picking an inexpensive stone, look for one of better quality, even if it costs a little more and takes more time to find. Remember that the gem you choose will say something about you as a person, signaling whether you are vivacious, tranquil, cool, or elegant. Attention should be paid to the cut of the gem.

Finally, you should know that there are some fine man-made stones that are both hard and colorful. Do not be put off by the distinction between natural and artificial stones. The latter can be quite beautiful and used to good effect.

January — *Garnet*

February — *Amethyst*

March — *Bloodstone*

April — *Diamond*

May — *Emerald* or *Jade*

June — *Pearl* or *Moonstone*

July — *Ruby*

August — *Sardonyx*

September — *Sapphire*

October — *Opal*

November — *Topaz*

December — *Turquoise*

GEM CHART

CHARACTERISTICS OF THE MAJOR STONES

Name of stone	Area of origin	Cut and characteristics	What to look for
DIAMOND	Brazil, Southwest Africa, The Congo; 92.5% come from Africa.	Crystals of pure carbon, the hardest of substances. Impervious to light, moisture. Brilliant cut is best.	1. The best are an intense white color that seems bluish. 2. White are next. 3. Plain yellow and brownish white in that order. Be sure that a stone does not have black spots, cracks, or a marred surface.
EMERALD	Colombia and Peru, South America. The Ural Mountains of USSR.	Beautiful green color. A high degree of hardness, but brittle and easily broken. Weakens in heat. Emerald or Cabochon cut.	1. Intense, clear, cold green color. 2. Absence of yellow or blue tint. 3. Diaphaneity (translucence). 4. Lack of white, brown, or black areas.
RUBY	Northern Mandalay in Burma, Thailand, Ceylon.	Burning red color. A high degree of hardness and durability. Usually step cut.	1. Deep and clear color. 2. High diaphaneity (translucence). 3. Few flaws. 4. Should not be too small. 5. Quality of form and cut.
SAPPHIRE	Mineralogically similar to the ruby. Found in Burma, Thailand, and Ceylon.	Generally harder and larger than the ruby. Surface is step cut, the back in a fine detailed cut.	1. Ideal color is a fine, clear sky blue. 2. Absence of muddiness or cloudiness, cracks, and stripes. 3. A certain degree of size.
JADE	The Kachin Plateau of Burma, Yunan Province in China, New Zealand, Wyoming.	There are two types — soft and hard — but they are almost identical. Fibrous and extremely tough. Usually an elliptical cabochon cut.	1. Feeling of depth and transparency of color. 2. Stones of poorer quality have areas touched with light brown and black, or a bluish green color. 3. The ideal shape is a full cone.
PEARL	Japanese cultured pearls: Japan, Australia, Iran. Natural pearls are a rarity and prices are prohibitive.	Carbonic acid and calcium. The least hard of stones, it is easily scratched, and weakens in acid.	1. Best are cream, pink, silver, or blue tints. 2. A seeming glow from within. 3. Perfect round shape. 4. Absence of scratches. 5. Over 7 to 8 mm. in diameter.
OPAL	Hungary, Australia, Mexico.	Translucence. Vivid red color. Australian stones are bluish. Mexican stones are reddish brown. Defects: break easily; weakened by light, heat, and alcohol.	1. Clear color tone without blemishes. 2. Large, full oval shape. 3. Absence of internal flaws (such flaws may be discovered by shining a beam of light on the stone).

CAT'S EYE	Ceylon, Brazil, Ural Mountains of USSR.	Brown stone that shines brilliantly when struck by light. High degree of hardness like the diamond and ruby. Has a "mysterious" quality about it.	1. Best are light brown, then yellow, gray, and deep sepia-laced brown. 2. Opalescent reflections and brightness. 3. A strong line running through the center of the stone.
STAR SAPPHIRE and STAR RUBY	Mysore and Madras in India, Tibet.	A characteristic six-pointed star appears when gem is struck by light. Cabochon cut, with the axis of the stone as the center.	1. Clear, deep color. 2. Reflected beams of light emerge vividly from center. 3. Absence of surface and internal flaws. 4. Fullness of volume.
ALEXANDRITE	Ural Mountains, USSR, Brazil.	A type of chrysoberyl. Appears emerald green in sunlight but red in artificial light.	Vivid color change from green to red when light changes from natural to artificial source.
AMETHYST	Bahia State in Brazil. Uruguay. Ural Mountains of USSR.	Usually flawed. Undergoes color change in sunlight and high heat. Cabochon or step cut.	1. Cold purple color without any black. 2. Well formed, full stones. 3. Absence of internal scratches or cracks.
TOPAZ	Brazil. Gifu and Shiga Prefectures in Japan.	An aluminum silicate. Yellow to yellow-brown in color. Defect: it changes color in sunlight and heat.	1. Yellow to yellow-brown in color. (Note: In Japan, yellow and smoky quartz are often sold as topaz.)
ZIRCON	Ceylon	Colorless and transparent, reminds one of diamonds, but very low degree of hardness. Changes color when exposed to sunlight.	Purest ones are colorless. Others are blue, green, yellow. Deep blue ones are popular. These are called blue zircons.
TURQUOISE	Western America. Iran. Arabia, Siberia.	Light blue, opaque gem. Soft and porous, thus easily marred and dirtied. Fades in sunlight and heat.	1. Best are light clear sky blue. 2. Big, full stones.
MOONSTONE	Ceylon. Madagascar. Korea.	A common stone of a semi-transparent white color that gives off a band of pearly blue light. Defect: softness.	Best ones are translucent milky white, emanate a brilliant pearly light, and have a full volume.
GARNET	Germany. Brazil. North and South America. India. Ceylon.	A bright, dark red stone. It may have touches of green — not blue-green — red, peach, and brown. It is fairly vulnerable and flaws are usual.	Best, from Bohemia in Germany, are ruby red in color. Italy produces a rare green garnet.
SARDONYX	Hokkaido, Sado Island, and the Hokuriku area of Japan. India. Brazil.	Includes both sardonyx and carnelian. When heat treated, the stone takes on the deep color of oxidized iron. May be dyed red, blue, or green. Basic coloration is alternating bands of brown and white.	A common stone. Look for equally spaced bands of color and beauty of pattern.
CORAL	South Seas, Japanese and other Pacific waters. Mediterranean waters.	Colors are all shades of pink, red, peach. Also pure white. Soft but fairly tough. Used in carvings, cabochons, beads. Twigs are used strung on chains for necklaces. Large branches are used for table ornaments. Polishes well.	Best is the pale, peach colored rose coral, followed by peach and reddish-white colored coral.

45

GEM CUTTING

The reason for cutting gems is to bring out the beauty of a stone. The rose, cabochon, brilliant, emerald, pear, marquise, and step cuts are among the commonly found styles. The brilliant cut is most effective with diamonds, the emerald cut with emeralds, and the cabochon cut with cat's eye, star ruby, and star sapphire. Other cuts are possible for a given type of stone. For example, the marquise cut or the square cut might be used on a diamond, depending on its shape. Again, depending on the stone in question, light coming from the top may be preferable in one case, while in another light entering from below would be desirable. In any case, the cut will be decided by the nature of the original stone, its depth of color, its thickness, and its shape. In turn, the cut chosen will determine the effect of the stone. Compare, for example, a round-cut diamond and a square-cut diamond. Study the way gems are cut by looking at displays in jewelry stores.

2-3. Types of gem cuts.

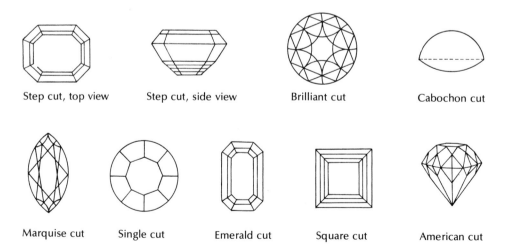

Step cut, top view   Step cut, side view   Brilliant cut   Cabochon cut

Marquise cut   Single cut   Emerald cut   Square cut   American cut

When purchasing a gem pay special attention to the light of the stone, its thickness, beauty of color, and quality of cut.

Gems that can take a cabochon cut do not require a fine cut. Generally these are gems that do not require the admission of bottom light, although there is a cabochon style for those that do. The cabochon style is considered somewhat informal, while more finely cut styles are dressy. Cabochon-cut stones include turquoise, opal, jade, sardonyx, black star, beryl, sapphire, star ruby, moonstone, lapis lazuli, amazonite, sodalite, malachite, coral, cat's eye, and certain garnets.

Stones requiring a more detailed cut include diamond, ruby, emerald, sapphire, alexandrite, topaz, zircon, some garnets, amethyst, and aquamarine. Occasionally it may be desirable to have these stones in a cabochon style, but this will depend on the design you have in mind and should be considered as special cases.

2-4. Types of cabochon cut.

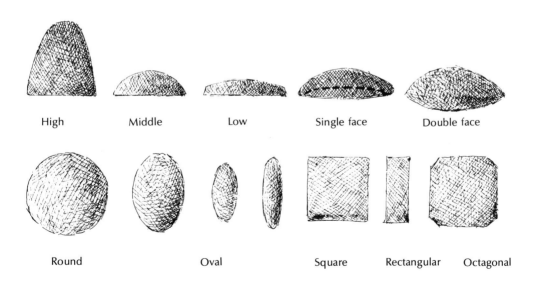

High   Middle   Low   Single face   Double face

Round   Oval   Square   Rectangular   Octagonal

2-5. An ideal diamond cut: 1/3 weak, 2/3 strong.

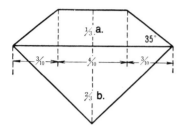

2-6. Faces of the brilliant cut.

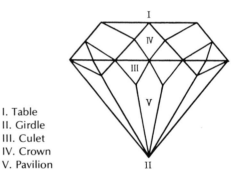

I. Table
II. Girdle
III. Culet
IV. Crown
V. Pavilion

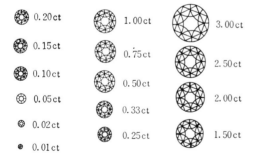

0.20 ct
0.15 ct
0.10 ct
0.05 ct
0.02 ct
0.01 ct

1.00 ct
0.75 ct
0.50 ct
0.33 ct
0.25 ct

3.00 ct
2.50 ct
2.00 ct
1.50 ct

2-7. Carat chart for diamonds (actual sizes are shown). The carat is a unit of weight equivalent to 0.2 gram. The chart above compares the size of the crown face of brilliant-cut diamonds.

THE COLORS OF DIAMONDS

The colors of diamonds are so subtle that they defy definition. The following, although inadequate, is an accepted description of diamonds according to color, listed in order of quality:

1. River — pure white touched with blue, called blue white.

2. Jager — pure blue tint, almost steel colored.

3. Wesselton — pure white without a yellowish tint, called snow white; the most popular stone.

4. Crystal — almost white but with a slightly yellowish tint; a medium quality stone.

5. Silver Cape — slightly yellowish; not a quality stone but has design possibilities.

There are also diamonds with decided hues, such as purple, pink, blue, canary, and black. These are called "fancies"; they are very rare and very costly.

SOME INEXPENSIVE GEM SUBSTITUTES

As stated earlier, the value of a gem is determined by its scarcity, hardness, beauty, index of refraction, and so forth. I would, however, like to approach the matter from another direction, that of designing and crafting jewelry.

I need not dwell on the beauty of emerald, rubies, and diamonds, but the cost of such gems is very high. Even if you choose to work with highly-priced stones you may find yourself unable to fully realize your idea. Remember that expense does not ensure fine work. My own experience has been that I work well with pearls, topaz, turquoise, agate, amazonite, lapis lazuli, garnet, moonstone, amethyst, opal, blue zircon, tourmaline, aquamarine, obsidian, malachite, hematite, rhodonite, tiger's eye, spinel, marble, coral, amber, smoky topaz, and jade, among others. Pearl, opal, and topaz are considered high-quality (precious) stones and are expensive, but the others listed on the chart are fairly common (semi-precious) and moderately priced. I have also found some natural uncut stones more attractive than beautifully cut ones. Some of the pieces shown in the color section at the beginning of this book use natural stones.

Glass may be used in place of a gem — fragments of a broken vase, an attractive bit of glass you have found and kept for its beauty. A favorite piece of mine is a ring I made with a scrap of glass I picked up in Greece some years ago. Washed-up sea shells, and even fish bones, have design possibilities. I have experimented with works using fragments of old rice bowls, combs, rusty iron, glass gems, fossils, seeds, and springs from old clocks. When you can take a discard, transform it, and, in a sense, breathe life into it once again, you will feel a glow known only to those who create beauty out of rejects. Baroque pearls (black, irregularly shaped), semi-circular pearls, and fresh-water pearls are comparatively inexpensive and may be used with excellent results.

HANDLING AND CARE OF GEMS

Although all gems have a certain degree of durability and ordinarily will not break or chip, they have other characteristics you should be aware of before dealing with them. The points listed below should be noted:

1. *Do not bring them close to fire.* Despite the fact that gems are produced by a fusion process within the earth, you may not apply direct heat to them. Diamonds are pure carbon crystal and will combust at a temperature of over 800 degrees. Before combusting, the surface will become white and opaque.

2. *Do not drop them or bang them:* Although diamonds are extremely hard, they are brittle and corners may break off. Emeralds are weak and break easily. Rubies and sapphires do not stand up well to shocks. Opals break and shatter. Garnets are brittle and must be handled with care.

3. *Stones that are weakened by acid and alcohol:* Pearls are weakened by acid, opals by both acid and alcohol. Do not wear rings set with these stones while working in the kitchen, bathing in a sulphur spring, etc. People who perspire a great deal should develop the habit of occasionally wiping their rings with a soft cloth.

4. *Stones that are weakened by sunlight:* If an opal is exposed to sunlight or heat for long periods, it will lose the moisture locked within it, and this may produce cracks. The color of turquoise fades easily in sunlight and heat; it is possible, however, to apply synthetic color as a touch up. Note that topaz, zircon, and amethyst are also subject to color changes in light and heat.

5. *Stones with easily marred surfaces:* The pearl is the softest gem and easiest to mar. Turquoise is comparatively soft, porous, easily marred and dirtied. Jade is not very hard on the scale, but it has viscosity and so may be considered among the strong gems; over a period of time the face of a jade stone may become worn and cloudy but can easily be returned to its former beauty by simple polishing.

6. *Gold, silver, and platinum settings:* There is nothing special to note about platinum, but gold and silver may be weakened by salt, therefore jewelry of these metals should be wiped clean with a soft cloth after being worn.

CLEANING GEM JEWELRY

In time the underside of the prongs that hold a gem in place, and the fine, narrow parts of a piece will collect dust and may appear dirty. Jewelry stores have ultrasonic cleaning equipment and you can have the jeweler clean your pieces for you. You may clean them yourself by washing with mild soap and water and wiping with a dry cloth.

REPAIRING GEM JEWELRY

Even when made with the greatest of care, in any gem jewelry a stone may become loose. If a small diamond comes loose and falls out, you can replace it yourself, but if the corner of a diamond breaks off, or if an emerald cracks, the stone must be cut to save it, and it must be reset. In addition to the time and expense involved, the stone will be reduced in size, which lowers its value and adds to the loss. In such case, instead of having the stone cut, it might be better to come up with a design that can accommodate the broken stone as it is.

TRADING GEMS

Should you grow tired of a gem and feel you would like something different, it is possible to trade in your stone as part payment on a larger, more expensive one of the same type; the trade-in price is usually quite good. If you deal with the same supplier from which you bought your original stone, the discount you can expect should be profitable. Make it a point to establish the trade-in discount before you close the original transaction. You should also remember that a small but good quality stone is more valuable in an exchange than a larger one of lower quality.

3.

BASIC TECHNIQUES FOR BEGINNERS

TOOLS AND MATERIALS

Your collection of tools is one of your most valuable possessions. A given tool will be used differently by different persons; the individual way in which you use a tool will ultimately make it yours and yours alone.

BEGINNING TOOLS

You will be using many types of tools as you go along, but you cannot expect to master them all immediately. You will gradually develop familiarity with them. Described next are tools you will need from the very beginning. Following this, we will learn about soldering techniques and the use of bunsen burners.

Whether your workshop is a small area in your apartment, a separate room, or a fully equipped workshop, if you are careful, you can enjoy the pleasures of jewelry making without injury to yourself or your surroundings.

Mallets — used for lightly tapping metal and in the first stages of chasing. These come both wood and plastic.

Hammers — used with gravers (chisels) and for pounding metal.

Resin base* — used in chasing. Made from pine resin and powdered earth. Must be softened by a burner before using.

Riveting hammer — used to pound metal.

Graver (chisel) — for chasing metal. Twelve or thirteen of these in various sizes are desirable. (See section on gravers.)

Anvil — for pounding, elongating, tempering, and impressing a seal on metal.

Rolling mill — while not essential at first, this item is highly recommended. It is extremely useful for elongating wire and sheet metal.

Hand drills — for making holes and wire twists. The wooden handles are usually hollow with a screw top, thus providing a convenient compartment for storing bits of various sizes.

Files — used to file metal, cut grooves, and smooth the cut edges of metal. Types range from rough to fine. About 10 is a good number to start with. Files will give you a great deal of service but they must be discarded when the teeth wear down.

Dapping die and Dapping ball punch — for fashioning bowl shaped pieces of metal for setting round stones. They come in 22 different sizes.

Bunsen burner — for soldering and tempering metal. Uses an air and gas mixture. (There are also hand-held torches, blow pipes, and foot-operated bellows to circulate air. Torches will be discussed later.)

Scrapers — for finishing rings and brooches. Used in place of a fine file.

Burnisher — along with the scraper, this tool brings out the gleam on the surface of metal.

Metal Brush — cleans dirt from metal. Used with sodium bicarbonate.

Tweezers — mainly used to hold metal when soldering, or acid dipping.

Compass — for making circles and measuring distances.

Ring-size stick (mandrel) — used to determine or to increase the size of a ring.

Cement — used mainly when setting pearls and round gems. Some cements come in two parts and must be mixed. To remove, once the cement has been applied, wash with hot water.

Sandpaper and emery paper — to smooth file marks on metal. These come in regular and in a waterproof. There are about 10 different types, but the best for your purposes is No. 0 to Nos. 20 or 30. Emery paper may be used with water or oil to clean tools.

Ring-size sets — wire loops in many sizes on a holder. Used to measure ring size before starting work.

Saw — for cutting metal. Rough and fine-tooth blades.

Metal shears — for cutting metal. Come with straight blades for cutting lines, curved blades for cutting curves, circles, etc.

Nippers (wire cutters) — to cut thick wire.

Pliers — for grasping small items and for bending wire.

---

*Prepared plastic bases can be purchased. Handmade pine resin bases are preferred by many jewelry craftsmen.

3-1. Tools.

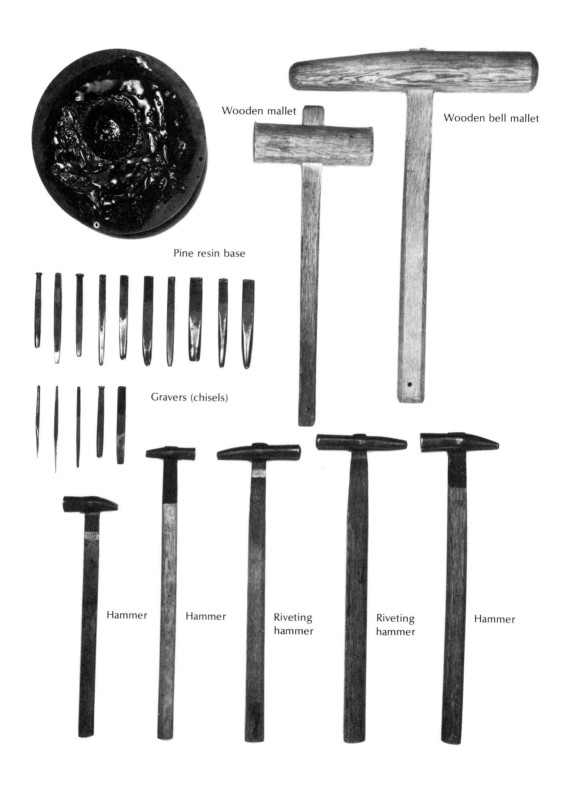

Wooden mallet

Wooden bell mallet

Pine resin base

Gravers (chisels)

Hammer   Hammer   Riveting hammer   Riveting hammer   Hammer

3-2. More tools.

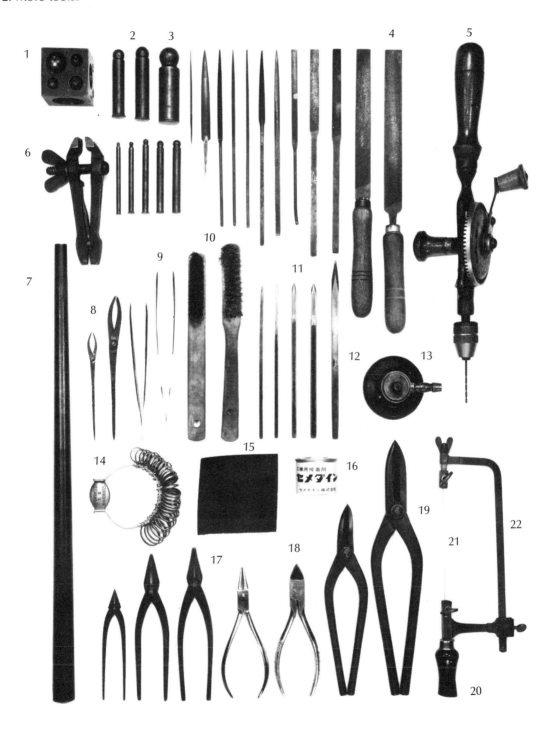

1. Dapping die. 2. Dapping ball punch. 3. Dapping ball punch. 4. Files. 5. Hand drill. 6. Hand vise. 7. Ring mandrel. 8. Compass. 9. Tweezers. 10. Brushes. 11. Fine scrapers. 12. Scrapers. 13. Bunsen burner. 14. Ring size set. 15. Sandpaper. 16. Epoxy. 17. Pliers. 18. Nippers (wire cutters). 19. Metal shears. 20. Saw. 21. Saw blade. 22. Saw frame.

3-3. Anvil. Used to pound and elongate metal. Scour the anvil with sandpaper to remove any rust and occasionally oil and wipe well.

3-4. Hand rolling mill. This is a fairly large one but smaller ones are available. Used mainly to elongate round and square wire, and for chasing.

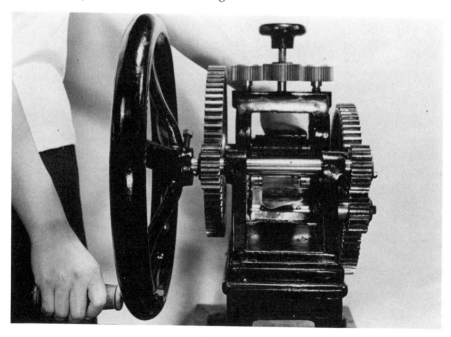

SOLDERING METHODS

Soldering is the operation of joining one piece of metal to another by placing a piece of soldering material between the pieces and then melting the solder. The secret of good soldering is in joining the pieces of metal as neatly as possible without leaving any gaps, and without the soldered spot being noticeable. When soldering, you will have to become familiar with the meaning of both the sound made when mixing the air and gas in your torch, and the color of the flame.

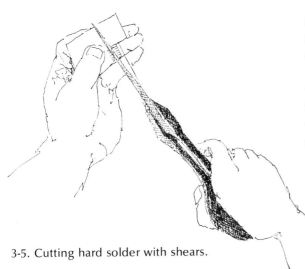

3-5. Cutting hard solder with shears.

HAND-HELD SOLDERING TORCH

The hand-held soldering torch is used both for soldering and for tempering metal. You can buy torches that run on either natural gas or propane. A bellows operated by a foot pedal is used with this torch. The advantage of the torch is that it enables you to concentrate your flame at a given spot, which makes it preferable to the Bunsen burner for soldering items with complex shapes. Since beginners, however, may have some difficulty using a torch, I suggest you start by using a Bunsen burner.

HOW TO MAKE A SIMPLE SILVER RING

Bend a strip of sheet silver into a circle. Place on an asbestos base. Apply borax and solder to the ends and press together. Now apply heat gradually until the moisture in the borax evaporates. The metal at the points to be joined will glow. Apply heat evenly to both ends until the solder melts and glows. The solder will flow to the hottest part of the metal.

When joining a small piece of metal to a large one, direct the heat to the largest part. If you heat the small part first the solder will flow there.

If the solder beads up as it hardens you have not applied sufficient heat. In time you will be able to tell if you are using the correct amount of heat by the color of the flame and its sound.

The borax acts as a flux, making the solder flow more quickly. Be sure to inspect your torch and rubber gas pipe before starting work, to make sure no cracks have developed, enabling gas to escape.

3-6. The flame.

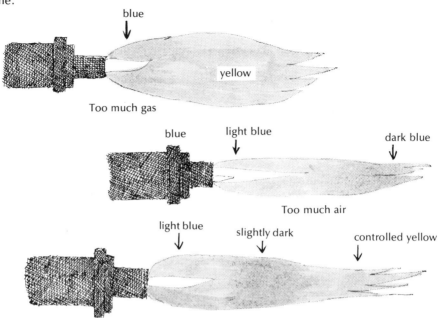

blue

yellow

Too much gas

blue   light blue   dark blue

Too much air

light blue   slightly dark   controlled yellow

Correct mix of gas and air

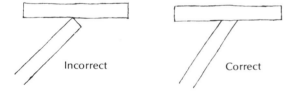

Incorrect   Correct

3-7. Position for soldering. When soldering, the joined parts should be bound as tightly as possible. If too much solder is used, adjustment later on will be a problem. Use it sparingly.

3-8. Placement of solder.

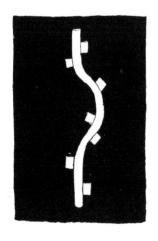

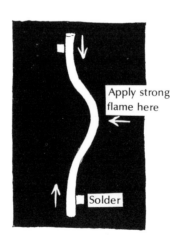

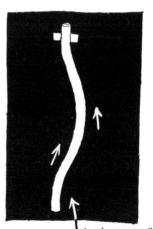

Apply strong flame here

Solder

Apply strong flame here

Incorrect   Correct   Correct

ACID DIPPING

When heating an alloy containing copper you produce copper oxide. This is black and undesirable in a piece of jewelry and should be removed by submersion in an acid dip.

To make the dipping solution you add sulfuric acid to water. Be sure to add the acid slowly, with the aid of a glass rod or similar instrument. If you pour acid without precautions it may splash and burn holes in your clothing and perhaps burn you. *If acid does get on your skin, wash it off with water immediately.* Acid dip may be mixed in a wide-mouth jar or bottle. You can protect yourself from acid splatters by using a wooden box with one open side. Place your jar or bottle inside as shown, when mixing your solution, to contain any splattering. Handle your piece with a curved tweezer. Wear old work clothes during this job, in case of an accidental splash.

The proportions of the solution are one part acid to ten parts water. Be accurate. If you put in too much acid, the surface of the silver will turn out rough and undesirable.

An acid dip should last for about 10 dippings but there is some variation. Be sure to keep the solutions you use for silver, gold, and platinum separate. Any solution used for a length of time will lose strength, and you will have to either add more sulfuric acid or mix a new batch.

NOTE. You should understand the basic preparation of acid-dipping solution, given here. Recently, however, an excellent product called *Super-Pickle Powder* has been formulated. With this, all you need to do is add water. It can be obtained from Gamzon Bros., Inc. and I. Shor Company (see "Suppliers" page 126). Recommended for beginners.

3-9. How to prepare acid dip.

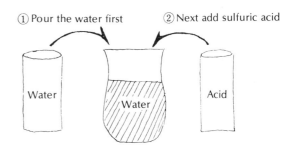

① Pour the water first   ② Next add sulfuric acid

Water

Water

Acid

Proportions: 10 parts water to one part sulfuric acid

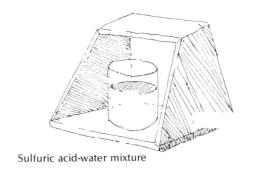

Sulfuric acid-water mixture

3-10. Wooden box with one open side.

LOST WAX CASTING

The lost wax method of precision casting is very old, dating back to ancient Egypt and China. It was also used in Japan to produce Buddhist statues and various implements. The lost wax technique involves the use of a modeling material called casting wax.

You begin by softening the wax. You can do this by soaking it in a basin of hot water. Fashion the wax into the form of the ring or brooch or whatever you have designed. The warmth of your hands will keep the wax soft while you are working with it. Don't make your piece any larger than necessary. (Remember, the bigger the piece, the more metal it will use and the more its cost will increase.) Fashion the wax to the size and thickness of the finished piece you are planning. The wax model you make will of course be much lighter than a metal piece, so do not add more wax simply because you think the model does not feel heavy enough. Also avoid making a model that is excessively thin and complicated, for this will make it difficult for the metal to flow easily when it is cast.

The great advantage of the lost wax method is that it enables you to produce a large number of pieces from a single model. The finished article will be slightly smaller than your wax model (about 10%). This method is particularly well suited for making jewelry that requires several pieces of the same pattern, such as cuff links and necklaces made by linking single pieces of the same design. It is far more efficient than handcrafting identical pieces over and over again.

When your wax model is complete, take it to a casting shop. Have at least five pieces cast from your model. Even if made of silver, this should not be too expensive. It usually takes about two or three weeks to have the casting done. During casting, the wax melts and is consumed by the heat used in the casting process, hence "lost wax." The casting shop will make a rubber mold from the wax model; you can use this if you want additional castings made. The finished cast pieces should have a clean texture, although you may have to remove a few projections of excess metal here and there. You can then work on the pieces by soldering, attaching stones, or whatever additional ornamentation you choose to add.

When casting in silver, an alloy of 5% copper is usually used, and, therefore, during soldering, cast silver will turn black. Do not be concerned. An acid dip will clean it up and restore its color.

JEWELERS' FILES

Files come in many different sizes and textures. You will need about 15 to 20 rough and fine files to begin with. Before using a file plunge it into charcoal ashes; this will prevent metal filings from getting stuck in the teeth of the file. Use rough files first and finish with fine ones. The correct way to file is to put force into outward or cutting stroke. The return stroke should be done lightly, without force.

The various types of files — round, oval, tapered, flat — differ in their use. For example, when cutting a groove in the surface of metal both a round file, tapering to a triangular tip, and a square file are used. You should try out each type, for there is no set rule that says you must use a particular file for a given job.

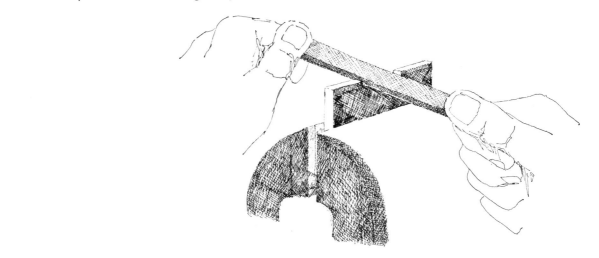

3-11. Correct way to hold file.

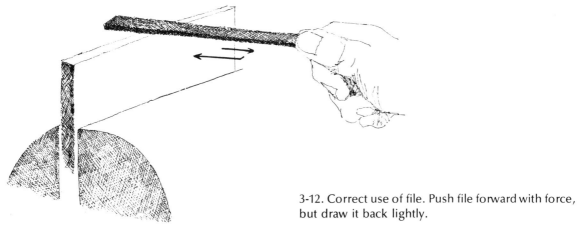

3-12. Correct use of file. Push file forward with force, but draw it back lightly.

3-13. Types of files.

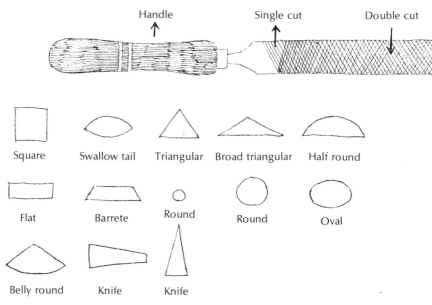

Handle   Single cut   Double cut

Square   Swallow tail   Triangular   Broad triangular   Half round

Flat   Barrete   Round   Round   Oval

Belly round   Knife   Knife

3-14. Cross sections of files.

3-15. When filing a small piece of metal hold it in a hand vise.

HOW TO MAKE SILVER BALLS

Occasionally a soldering job will turn out poorly. If you apply too much heat or cut the flame too late the silver will melt and become muddy. However, if you keep the flame on, the silver will begin to form a ball. You can make use of this phenomenon to make decorative silver balls, which can be used in various ways. Cut a piece of round or square wire, apply a flame to the wire as you rotate it. At the metal's melting point a ball will form at the end of the wire. Pure silver, rather than the 5% copper alloy, makes prettier balls.

DECORATIVE USES OF MELTED METAL

Another interesting material may be formed during the tempering of sheet metal and wire (see **Page 64**). If you apply more heat than necessary for tempering, the metal will melt. If this happens, withdraw the metal from the flame — you may find metal in this state is an attractive medium to work with. I often use such muddy, melted silver in brooches and rings. Although completed works that make use of such melted metal look as though they were made by the lost wax method, the delicate effect achieved by melting narrow pieces of wire cannot be produced by lost wax techniques. As with silver balls, I suggest that pure silver, rather than the 5% copper alloy, will give a better effect.

You could finish your piece by simply oxidizing the surface, or by plating it with gold or rhodium.

3-16. Making silver balls.

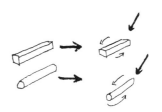

Square and round silver wire

Applying a strong flame

Rotate until a ball forms and withdraw flame

Heat other end of wire in strong flame until ball forms, then withdraw quickly

TEMPERING

Bending, stretching, and beating sheet metal
or wire may stiffen, break, and crack it. You
can soften your material by heating it, a process called *tempering*. Use a soft, almost yellow flame with little air for tempering. A piece
may be tempered any number of times while
you are working on it, but you should not
temper it again once it is finished. The final
touches on a piece should be done with a
scraper and a burnisher.

If you try to temper metal with too strong a
flame it may melt, as noted before. It will take a
certain amount of experience before you can
judge when the metal is sufficiently tempered
and when to cut the heat.

3-17. Tempering a long roll of silver wire. Sufficient
tempering will be achieved by a weak flame evenly
applied to the entire roll.

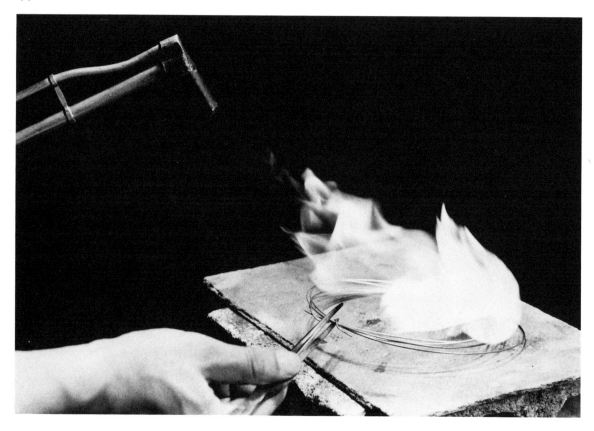

USING A JEWELER'S SAW

The jeweler's saw is an indispensable tool, but using one is not as easy as it may seem. Learn to use long, even strokes and maintain a light, regular rhythm. While using the saw, hold it vertically (see picture) and cut lightly, following the lines of your design. Follow the lines as closely as possible, moving the saw away from you. If you use your saw correctly you will not need to do much filing. Occasionally coat the blade with wax, which will make it slide more easily. No. 00 to No. 2 are the most often used blade sizes. No. 00 is best for doing openwork.

You will probably break many saw blades at first, but this is the only way to gain skill in the use of a saw.

Saw and drill are both used when doing openwork. Begin by making a hole with your drill. Then pass the blade of your saw through the hole, lock the blade into the frame, and proceed to cut away your design. For narrow parts of the design use a narrow bit. A hand-sawed, openwork piece will be far more attractive than even a similar pattern die-stamped by machine could possibly be.

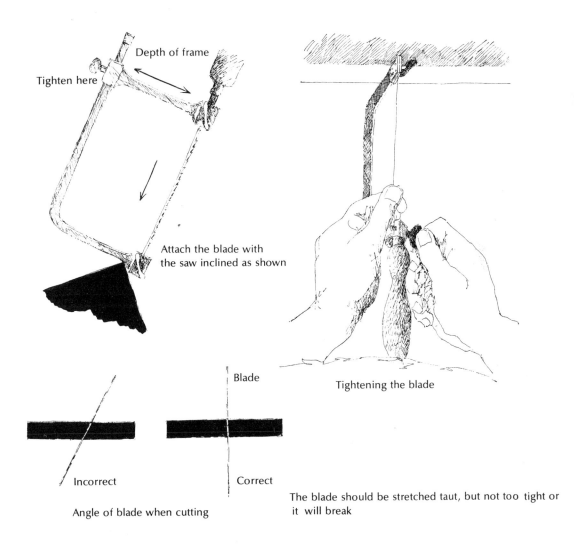

Depth of frame

Tighten here

Attach the blade with the saw inclined as shown

Tightening the blade

Blade

Incorrect

Correct

Angle of blade when cutting

The blade should be stretched taut, but not too tight or it will break

3-18. How to use jeweler's saws.

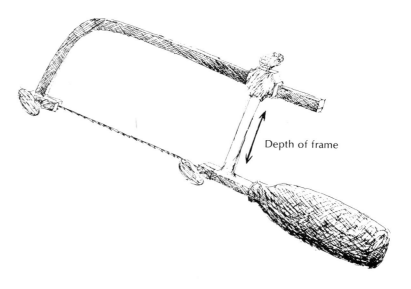

3-19. Each saw has its own depth of frame. A shallow depth of frame is sufficient for rings and small brooches. Saws having a sizable depth of frame are good for cutting larger brooches, bracelets, etc.

3-20. Drill a hole, then pass the saw blade through, lock it in, and cut away the interior parts of the design. Note the grip on the saw. Be sure to catch the pieces you cut away.

DRILLING HOLES

Before drilling a hole, mark the spot with a
sharp, pointed piece of metal (chisel). Insert a
suitable bit in the drill chuck, tighten the chuck
by turning it clockwise (page 68).

Narrow bits tend to break easily. They
should be used as little as possible, and with
care, especially after the bit has passed
through the hole in the metal. Bits also come in
medium and large sizes.

Very large bits are not necessary for jewelry
making. A fairly narrow bit is used when cutting patterns and doing openwork. Drills are
also used to make holes in pearls; a pearl is
held in place in a piece of equipment called a
pearl-drilling jig (not shown).

3-21. Use two nails to anchor your metal sheet.
Otherwise it may turn with the drill.

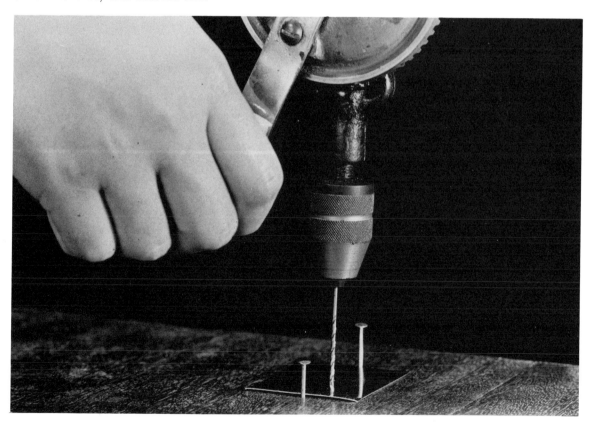

3-22. First mark position of hole with a sharp, pointed graver as shown.

3-23. How to hold the drill.

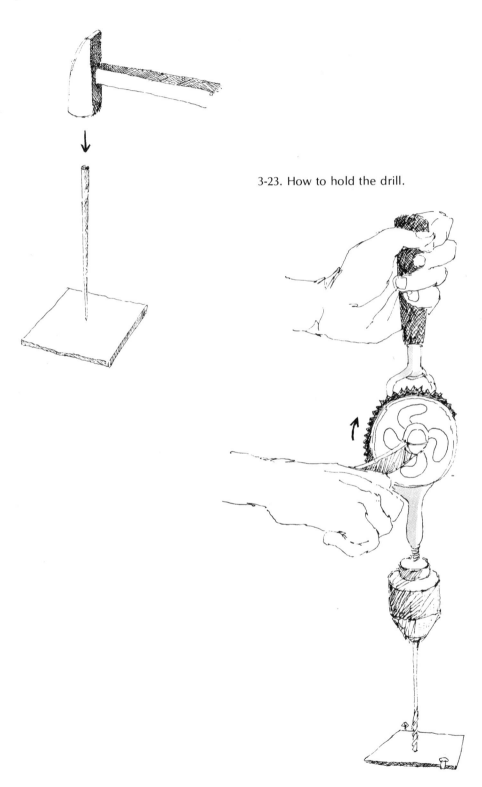

MAKING WIRE TWISTS

To make a wire twist, begin by tempering a length of wire. Bend the wire in half, hook the center onto a nail and insert the two ends into the chuck of a hand drill. When you turn the drill clockwise the wire will begin to form a twist. Continue tempering the wire and twisting it until the whole length is finished. If your twists are too tight the wire will form a packed knot. If too relaxed, the twists will be loose.

If your twist is too long it may tear in the middle, so be careful. You can use your completed twist in various ways. To mention only one, you might take a twist, bend it in two, and try twisting it again.

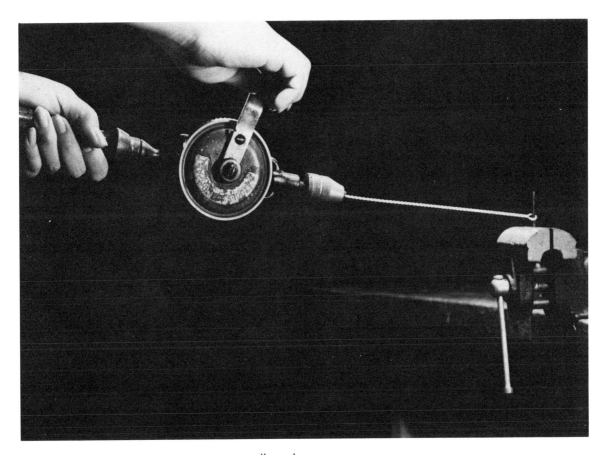

3-24. When making a twist, remove repeatedly and temper it.

HOW TO MAKE A PINE RESIN BASE*

First place an iron pot on a low flame and melt the resin. Stir in powdered earth a little at a time, making sure to blend well. Add vegetable oil, which provides viscosity. Use a wooden spoon to mix the resin compound. Be very careful, as *hot resin can cause serious burns*. The amount of oil you will need varies with the temperature. In cool weather use a bit more oil, in warm weather use a bit less.

3-25. How to make a pine resin base.

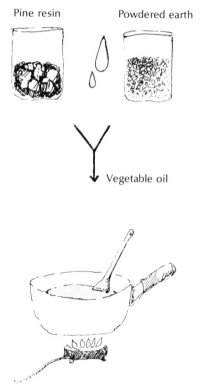

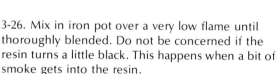

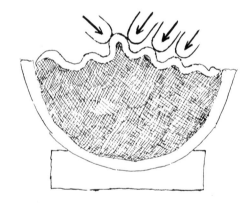

3-27. Cross section of a resin base. Soften with a burner. Concentrate in center.

3-26. Mix in iron pot over a very low flame until thoroughly blended. Do not be concerned if the resin turns a little black. This happens when a bit of smoke gets into the resin.

The proportions given below are enough for one resin base.

10 ounces of powdered earth
4 ounces of pine resin
2-3 teaspoons of vegetable oil

*Bases made of plastic can be purchased.

70

HOW TO STRETCH WIRE

Wire may be narrowed in a drawplate. If you buy all your wire in the various sizes you want, your supply can begin to run into money. It is cheaper to buy fairly thick wire and narrow it yourself to the size you want. You might buy three different sizes of wire, for example. 0.4 mm., 1.0 mm., and 1.8 mm. thicknesses (gauges), and then narrow them to intermediate sizes as needed.

A drawplate is still another indispensable tool. You can buy drawplates with differently shaped holes (round, square, etc.). As shown in the diagram opposite, wire is pulled through the drawplate to narrow it. First file the end of the wire to a point with a rough file, then push this end through the proper hole in the drawplate, grip with snub-nose pliers and pull it through. Remember to temper the wire now and then to soften it and prevent breaking. Keep drawing the wire through successive holes in the plate until you achieve the dimension desired.

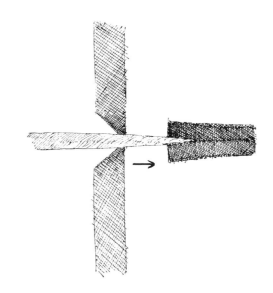

3-28. File end of wire to a point. Push through a hole in the drawplate, grasp with snub-nose pliers. Drawing shows cross section.

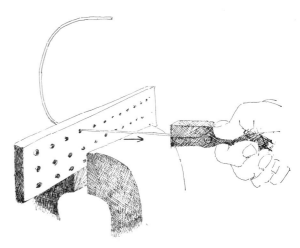

3-29. Pulling wire through the drawplate.

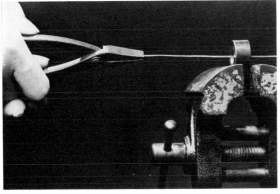

3-30. Stretching silver wire through a drawplate held in a vise. Temper occasionally.

HOW TO MAKE PIPE WIRE

Pipe wire is necessary to make prongs that hold gems in place, and is very useful for ornamentation. (See ring shown below.)

Square and round pipe wire is available at suppliers, but making your own is much less expensive.

Procedure

1. Cut a sheet of metal equal to the overall measurement of the pipe wire you want to make. The width of the sheet must be three times the diameter of the pipe. The thickness of the sheet will be the thickness of the wall of the pipe. Be sure to file the ends exactly straight.

2. Taper one end of the sheet so it can be inserted into a drawplate after it has been curved.

3. Temper the sheet and curve it on a grooved design block or an anvil.

4. Insert the sheet in a drawplate and pull. Stretch to desired length. Trim off tapered end.

5. Before joining the sides of the pipe, file or saw them so they will join cleanly. Solder at this point, using 3% to 5% alloy.

3-31. Ring with a pipe wire motif. Turquoise are set into the ends of the wire. Silver with a rhodium finish.

3-32. Step-by-step diagram for making pipe wire.

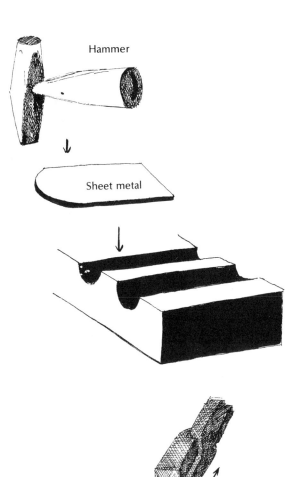

Hammer

Sheet metal

Grooved design block

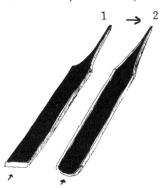

Sheet metal strip with end tapered

1 → 2

Tapered strip after curving on grooved block

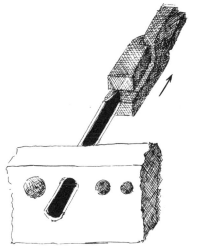

Stretching to desired size in drawplate

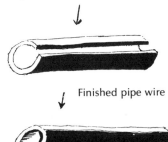

Trim tapered end, then solder to a clean fit, using hardest flowing solder (3% - 5%)

Finished pipe wire

PLIERS, NIPPERS (WIRE CUTTERS), AND SHEARS

Long-nose pliers are used mainly to bend metal wire and sheeting. Blunt-nose pliers have great gripping power and are used to hold metal above an anvil and to pull wire through a drawplate.

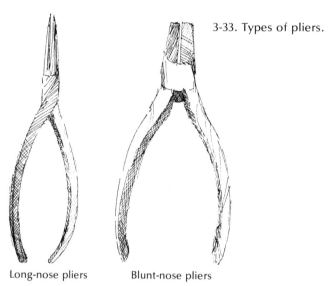

3-33. Types of pliers.

Long-nose pliers   Blunt-nose pliers

3-34. Nippers are used to cut wire.

3-35. Straight-edge shears for cutting straight lines.

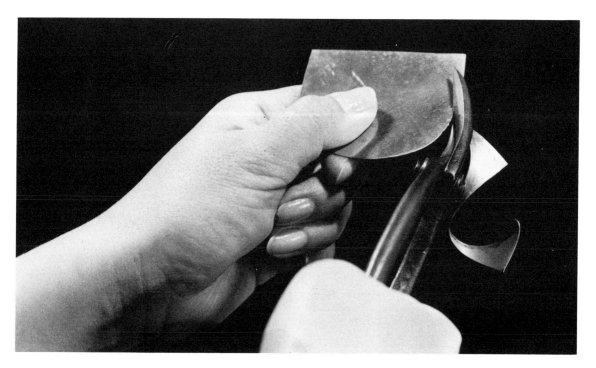

3-36. Curved-edge shears for curved lines.

HOW TO MAKE SIMPLE GRAVERS (CHISELS)

Gravers (chisels) are required tools for *chasing*, a fundamental technique of jewelry making much used in fashioning brooches, rings, and bracelets. Gravers are available from supply houses, but you can make your own set of gravers by simply purchasing 10 to 15 square carbon steel rods that can be cut and filed.

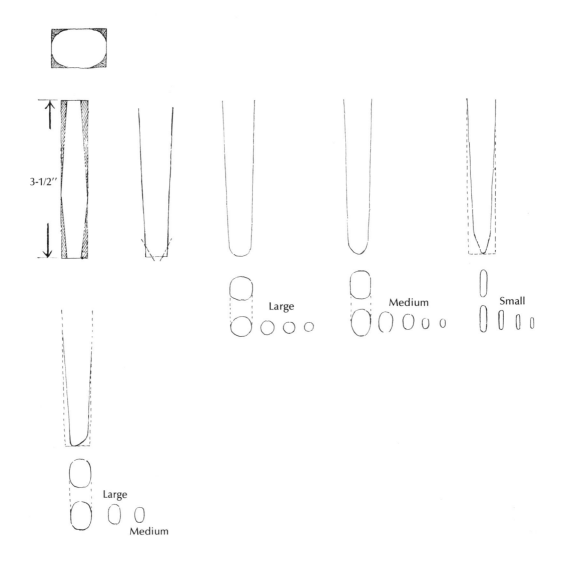

3-37. Types of gravers (chisels). Carbon steel is used to make gravers. There are several different types used for engraving, embossing, and chasing.

Cut the rods to a length of about three or four inches. Temper until red hot and set on your anvil to cool. Next, round off the square sides of the rods, which will make them more comfortable to handle. From a point about a third of the way up file the rod so it tapers to a point. Begin by using a rough file, progress to finer files, and finish by polishing with sandpaper. Next, while holding the graver in a pincer, heat the tip until it turns red-brown in color, remove from the flame, and quickly plunge into a jar of cool water prepared beforehand. This will harden the point. Wipe with a cloth and polish well with metal cleaner.

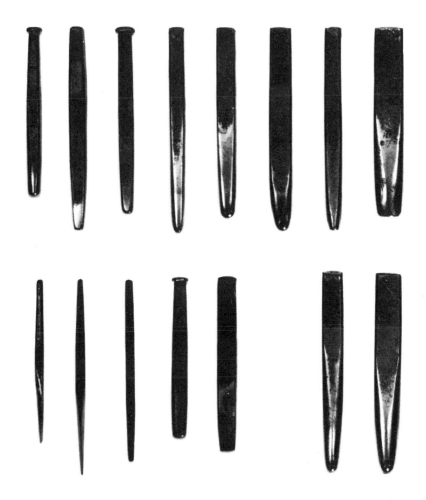

3-38. A variety of handcrafted gravers.

CHASING TECHNIQUES

Chasing involves tempering, the use of a resin base, and a method of raising and depressing metal by striking a graver with a hammer to create a desired pattern. This time-honored technique is indispensable to the craft of jewelry making. In chasing, you work freely on a sheet of hard metal and you can endow the smooth metal with a special kind of elegance and liveliness. Although chasing is sometimes thought to give a piece an antique look, it more often contributes an extra dimension in creating original modern jewelry of true distinction.

Use sheet metal (copper or silver) about 1 mm. thick, except in special cases.

Procedure

1. Temper your metal sheet. (See earlier section on tempering.)

2. Execute your design on drawing paper. Transfer it to tracing paper. Paste the tracing-paper pattern on the metal. Then, with a pointed rod or scriber and hammer, tap lightly along the lines of your design. This should make a clear pattern on the metal.

3. After transferring the pattern, coat the back of the metal with vegetable oil to facilitate a smooth contact between the resin base and the metal on which you will do the chasing.

Next, place the metal sheet on the resin base (oiled side down) and, while warming from above with a small flame from your burner, press the sheet firmly onto the resin. *Be especially careful not to get any melted resin on your fingers.*

4. Now you are ready to start the chasing. Begin work on spots where you can use a fairly large graver. The resin will cool while you are working, and your sheet may peel off. If it does, again apply a weak flame to the sheet. You should try to maintain the resin at a level of heat about equivalent to body temperature.

When you are finished with the large graver, use a smaller one and then move on to finer ones as needed. Remember to work from the general to the detailed. If you start doing the fine work first you may end up by breaking the sheet. Another matter to watch for: the sheet may warp while you are doing the chasing. Should this happen, place it on your anvil and lightly tap it back into shape.

To remove the sheet from the resin, again heat from above with a burner, then grip it at one side with pliers and pull it off. Any resin that sticks to the metal can be wiped off with a rag while it is still hot, or rubbed off with the nose of your pliers after it has cooled. At this point the pattern should be visible.

5. Temper the sheet, as it will be quite stiff by now. Give the sheet an acid dip and then correct any warping (as described in 3. above). Be careful not to injure the pattern. Turn the piece face down on a softened resin base. Start chasing the spots you want to have in highest relief. Be careful not to chase it too much, since this could tear the sheet. Next, coat the back with oil and again attach it to the resin, face up. Be sure that the sheet and resin fit together well, for air pockets can easily form. If they do, the sheet will cave in while you are working on it and ruin the piece.

6. Continue chasing the piece in the center and along the sides. As you do, the form will begin to come to life beneath your graver. Be sure to hold the graver perpendicular to your work. Heat the resin from above, under the areas you want raised, and tap around them with your graver to get the raised effect. For areas you want depressed, allow the resin at these spots to cool, then tap lightly. If you puncture the piece your work will all be wasted. To avoid this, regularly hammer the metal down around the area you are working on so that the center will be forced up. Do not forget to temper the piece.

7. Once you have completed the chasing, you must decide how you are going to finish the piece. This part of your work should enhance the effect you want the piece to create. There are a number of choices for finishing; for example, you can plate it with gold, or, if it is a silver piece, give it an antique look.

Detailed illustrated instructions for creating a chased brooch appear on the following eight pages.

HOW TO CREATE A CHASED BROOCH

3-39. First execute your design on paper. When you are satisfied with it, transfer to tracing paper.

3-40. Paste the tracing paper copy onto the metal and perforate lines of your design. The tracing paper will burn away when you temper the metal, so don't be concerned about it.

3-41. Warm the resin base with a burner. Set the metal with the tracing paper design on top of it, then pound around the edges with a riveting hammer until the center puffs up.

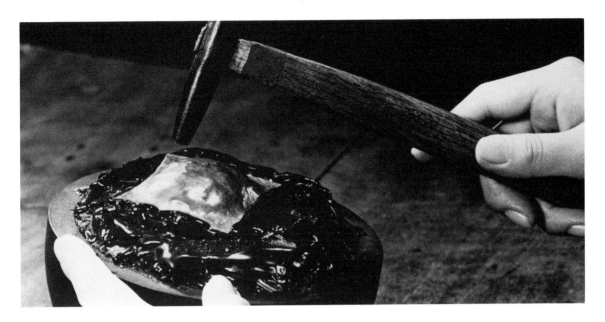

3-42. Start by chasing the piece first with a large graver.

3-43. Use finer gravers for the finer parts. Work gently. If you hit the metal too hard you may break it.

3-44. Using a sharp, pointed graver follow the outline of the brooch and cut away the surrounding metal.

3-45. Start work on the face.

3-46. Finish face.

3-47,-48. Attach a sheet of metal to the back of the completed brooch face. To do this, tie the two pieces together with metal wire and solder. Cut away the unnecessary metal on the back to make the brooch lighter and save metal. Trim with a saw and finish with a file.

3-49. Next, impress the name of the metal and your seal on the back of the brooch. You can have a seal with your own design made by your materials supplier. Attach clasp with solder.

3-50. Coat with acid and let stand for about 10 minutes, then rinse well. Check the piece carefully to make sure it is completely clean.

3-51. Oxidize the surface with a mixture of gold chloride and high quality pure alcohol. Polish with wax metal cleaner. Finally, set the clasp pin and your brooch is finished.

Facing page

3-52. Finished brooch.

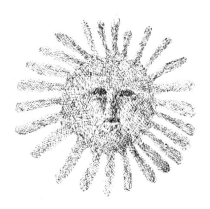

SETTING STONES

You should know how to set stones. Precious gems like rubies, emeralds, sapphires, diamonds, and opals should be set by a specialist, but semi-precious and lesser stones can be set even by a beginner.

There are two major ways of setting stones: with prongs or with ornamental borders. There are several types of prong sets, such as 4-prong, 6-prong (or Tiffany style), 8-prong, Chrysanthemum (with many prongs suggesting the petals of the chrysanthemum), and the angular prong, which grips the angles of the stone. In general, the fewer the number of prongs, the larger the stone appears to be. In multiple-prong settings, the prongs are narrower. The 4-prong set is in favor at this time.

The prong set is the style most often used in diamond rings. This set gives a light feeling in tune with finely-cut stones, and it has a contemporary air. It is also considered formal, whereas the ornamental border setting seems more suitable for general wear.

Although setting a stone with an ornamental border is simple enough for a beginner to do, if you are working with a soft stone, or with a valuable one that requires a prong set, have a specialist do the job for you.

3-53. To set a stone in an ornamental border tap lightly all around the border, using a narrow pointed graver.

3-54. An ancient European crucifix encrusted with many stones set in ornamental borders.

SETTING STONES IN ORNAMENTAL BORDERS

Setting gems in ornamental borders is an old technique, long used in handcrafted rings and brooches. Many examples may be seen in museums and European churches, used for setting both cabochon-cut stones and rough, angular uncut stones. While setting with ornamental borders is not regarded as suitable for the precious stones, as noted above, it gives a handsome look to more ordinary cabochon-cut stones. On the other hand, there is no strict rule that says you must use a prong set for the more expensive gems; for example, there is a dish setting, similar to the ornamental border, that is often used for diamonds and the other precious stones. This is done by placing a gem into a prepared dish-shaped depression and pushing the surrounding metal along the border of the gem. It looks much like the ornamental border setting. If the gem is large however, a prong set is best. But whatever type of setting you choose, it must essentially contribute to the aura of the piece as a whole.

See "Ring, constructed" page 99.

3-55. Step-by-step diagrams for making ornamental border settings.

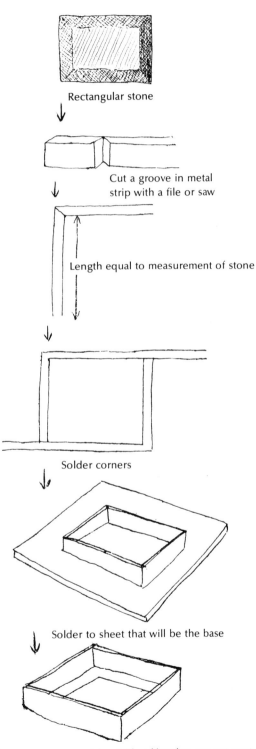

Rectangular stone

Cut a groove in metal strip with a file or saw

Length equal to measurement of stone

Solder corners

Solder to sheet that will be the base

Cut away excess metal outside of border, cut out center, leaving a 2 mm. band all around

3-56. Octagonal border.

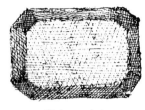

Octagonal stone

Cut grooves with file and bend with pliers

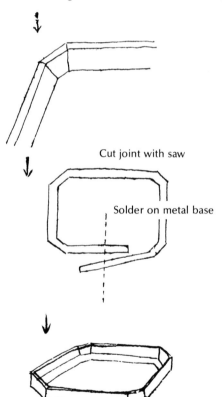

Cut joint with saw

Solder on metal base

Cut away center of base,
leaving 2 mm. band

3-57. Cabochon border.

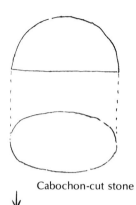

Cabochon-cut stone

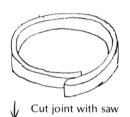

Cut joint with saw

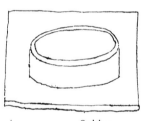

Solder

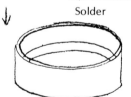

Cut out center of base,
leaving 1-2 mm. band

SETTING PEARLS AND ROUND STONES

A pearl may be set with prongs. While this permits you to set it without drilling a hole into it, the prongs will intrude upon the beauty of the pearl. Another way to set a pearl is to drill a hole, insert a post and secure it with cement. Of course, when you drill a hole in it, you are creating a flaw in the pearl, but remember that a prong setting for a pearl may also flaw its beauty.

Always choose a flawed spot to drill the hole. Insert the stone in a pearl-drill jig, and hand drill a hole with the appropriate size bit. You can also use an electric drill.

Procedure

1. Make a bowl-shaped piece of metal to hold the pearl. It should be done so that the metal will not be visible when you look at the attached pearl from above.
2. Make a post of square wire. Insert in pearl. Twist the post so that the pearl will not slip. Make a hole in the center of the bowl, insert end of the post and solder in place.
3. Apply a binding agent (epoxy or industrial cement). Set the pearl so that it sits securely in the bowl.

3-58. Step-by-step diagrams for setting pearls and round stones.

Make a bowl using the appropriate sized dapping ball punch

Drill hole in center, insert post and solder

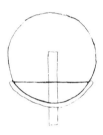

Set stone with binding agent (To remove, if necessary, flush with hot water)

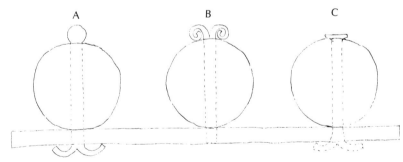

Example A: To set a stone with a hole completely through it, make a ball at the exposed end of the post, split the concealed end at bottom and spread apart as shown in diagram

Example B: An alternative to the method described in example A is to solder the concealed end, cut a groove in the exposed end, and spread apart.

Example C: This is similar to example A, but be sure that the exposed end conceals the hole in the stone

3-59. Method for making a bowl.

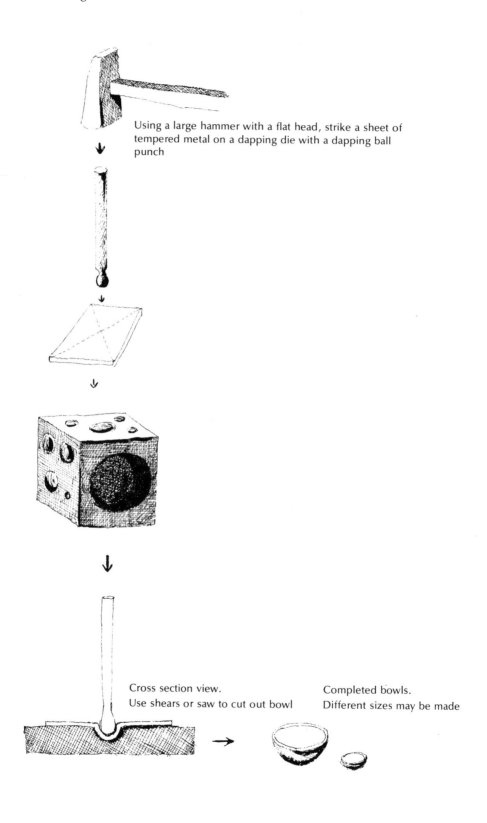

Using a large hammer with a flat head, strike a sheet of tempered metal on a dapping die with a dapping ball punch

Cross section view.
Use shears or saw to cut out bowl

Completed bowls.
Different sizes may be made

FUNDAMENTAL PRINCIPLES OF DESIGN

Since designing jewelry is an art, imagination as well as technique and manual skill are essential. Train yourself to see and to feel. In a world so full of a number of things, the seeing eye will discover design inspiration everywhere. There is excitement in discovering design possibilities in the simple shapes and patterns of everyday life — the stark symmetry of factory roofs (overleaf), the balance and texture of chocolate bars (page 96), a child's Halloween costume (page 95), geometry (circles and squares, page 97), the intricacies of Egyptian hieroglyphics noted during a museum trip (page 97), even a fish platter at the end of a well enjoyed meal (page 105), faces (pages 104, 105).

The myriad everchanging forms in nature offer ideas without end. Explore architecture and art. Let your imagination soar while listening to music. Observe the pure patterns to be found in music scores.

If you find original designing hard going at first, begin by studying pieces done by professionals. Try adding personal touches to classic designs. You will soon have the urge to do completely original creations that bear the stamp of your own personal vision.

Always remember that jewelry is made to be worn and must enhance the wearer. Beware of making pieces that are too big or too heavy. Here are some basic principles of design you should always keep in mind:

1. Ask yourself when and where the piece will be worn before you begin designing it. Make as many sketches of the piece as necessary. When working with stones, first consider whether they are casual — turquoise, certain opals, lapis lazuli, amethyst (uncut cabochon), onyx, sodalite — or dressy: diamond, ruby, sapphire, jade, cut amethyst, emerald, and opal.

2. Size depends on taste. Unless you are striving for a special effect do not make your pieces on too large a scale.

3. Complete your design on paper before starting work on it, or you will run the risk of forgetting and so seriously altering your original idea as you proceed. Work according to a set plan.

4. Weight. Always remember that jewelry is something you wear. Rings and earrings that are uncomfortably heavy, brooches that pull clothing, chains and pendants that are burdensome fail as pieces of jewelry. Strive for a feeling of lightness.

5. Avoid waste in design. Aim for simplicity.

6. You may, perhaps now and then, create pieces while in the grip of an emotion. They may show technical mastery but fail as total conceptions. You should value such pieces for the intimate sensation they represent.

7. Let your own taste decide such matters as balance or imbalance: left-right symmetry, or asymmetry.

8. Findings. Give practical thought to clasps, chain joints, and such. Make sure they are easy to use.

9. Finally, you will have to decide how to finish your piece, for example, whether to polish or oxidize the surface, plate it with gold, give it a shiny or a matte surface, combine techniques, and so on.

3-60. The idea for the piece shown above came from
aligned factory roofs, their straight short lines creating a modernistic pattern. Silver brooch, oxidized
finish.

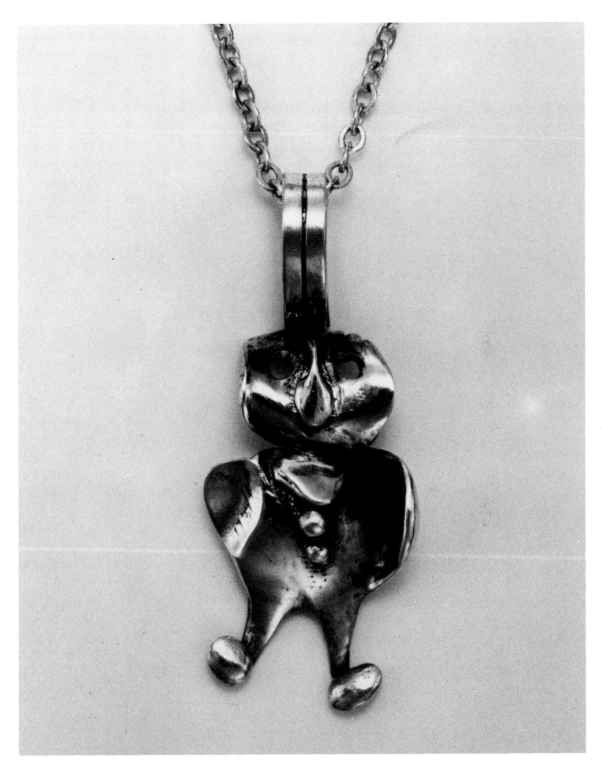

3-61. Here is an impish little demon created by the lost wax method. This piece can be used as a pendant, or as a key holder. Silver with oxidized finish.

Top. 3-63. A handsome openwork ring suggested by Egyptian hieroglyphics. Silver, oxidized silver finish.

3-62. Design for this brooch was inspired by a chocolate bar! Can be used as a pendant or as a brooch. Silver, oxidized silver finish.

Bottom. 3-64. A theme of circular and square shapes is employed in this unusual ring that seems to change according to the wearer's mood.

SEALS

In addition to stamps for names of the metals used, you can order a personal seal or trademark stamp with your name or sign on it. The cost of the stamp varies with the design, so consult your materials dealer.

The large initial at the top of the right-hand column is my seal. It is a combination of the *T* of Takashi and the *W* of Wada. The oval border represents a gem, pendant, or brooch.

The seal at left is a mark I use on cases, the border represents a gem or pendant encircling a stylized *W* for Wada.

Note the other examples of seals shown on this page.

3-65. A variety of seal designs.

4.

CREATING JEWELRY

RINGS, CONSTRUCTED (1)

How you make a ring will of course depend on your design. If you are using a stone, let it decide the feeling of the ring as a whole. The method for making rings described here is a basic one you should practice. Learn it, and you can then adapt it for different designs. Begin working around the stone and proceed in the order described below.

Procedure for making an ornamental border

1. With a hand roller flatten 1 to 1.2 mm. round or square wire. Flattened, it will be about 0.4 to 0.6 mm. thick.
2. Lightly temper the flattened wire and, using blunt-nose pliers, wrap it around your stone to determine size needed, then cut to size with a saw or metal shears. File the ends well — this is done to eliminate slack. Solder the ends together on the inside, using 3% or 5% alloy solder. File off any excess solder.
3. Now place the frame you have just made on a 0.5 mm. thick sheet. Apply borax around it and solder to the sheet with 5% alloy solder. Place the solder in one spot, or, in smaller amounts, in two places. Apply flame until solder flows around. Cut away the inside of the sheet, leaving a band about 1 mm. all around. Smooth the cut edge of the band with a fine file. Next, file the top outside edge of the border frame to a 45-degree angle.
4. Make a wire twist from 0.4 to 0.5 mm. round wire (see the section on wire twists). The tightness of the twist should suit your overall design. Lightly temper the border, cut the wire

twist to fit around the border, but make it a bit smaller to ensure a tight fit. Join the ends of the twist with solder and place it on your anvil. Insert the border face up into the ring-shaped twist and press it down hard until the bottom edge of the border makes contact with the anvil. Turn the assembled piece upside down and solder.
5. Next, cut a piece of 1.5 mm. thick sheet silver to a length equaling the circumference of the stone plus about 1.5 mm. more. This will serve as the supporting base of the stone. Temper well and bend with pliers so that stone rides it exactly. If you are using an oval stone, bend the base into an oval shape. Solder the ends of the base together and solder to a bottom sheet. Cut a hole in the bottom.
6. Now you are ready to ornament the base. Cut a pattern into the base with a three-square file, rotating the base as you turn. Before you start, make a sketch of your decorative pattern as a guide.

Since the base is made of 1.5 mm. thick sheet you may file fairly deep grooves. This will make the finished pattern more effective. Next, solder the base and the ornamental border together.
7. Now you must make the shank of the ring, which is the part that fits around your finger. To make an average No. 12-size ring cut a 50 mm. length of 4 mm. X 4 mm. square wire, temper and curve it on a grooved design block. File the ends so they fit neatly, then solder. Round the corners of the band with rough file, temper lightly, pass it onto a ring mandrel. Tap to the size No. 12 mark. Remove, clean up the surface with a narrow file, and finish with a

scraper and burnisher. The completed shank is similar in form to a plain wedding band. It is a basic form but can be worked by you to produce some interesting effects, such as cutting it in two, or cutting part way through as shown in a previous diagram.

8. The final step. Tie the top mounting to the shank with binding wire, then solder from the underside. As you will not be using your torch again, the ring can now be cleaned with acid and polished thoroughly with a metal brush, using water and soap or sodium bicarbonate. In good light, rub on a silver antiquing solution (composed of silver chloride and alcohol), using a worn out brush with the bristles cut in half. The metal will become completely black. When dry, give the ring a light coating of iodine. The oxidized antique surface in the grooves will remain black while the rest of the metal will shine. Polish with metal cleaner and a cloth to bring out the contrast between the dark design and the bright surface. Carefully finish the bright surface with fine sandpaper and a burnisher. You may wish to finish the ring with rhodium or gold plate but do consider the effect it will have on the whole piece. You should have plating done for you.

4-1. Step-by-step diagrams for constructed rings.

Stone

Make an ornamental border to set stone

Make a wire twist and solder to border

Work ornamentation with a file on the base piece that will hold the stone

The shank

If the ring size happens to be small, build a bridge by soldering silver balls between the base of the setting and the shank

Finished ring

Other possibilities. Here are some ideas for ornamentation without the use of stones

4-2. How to curve the ring shank.

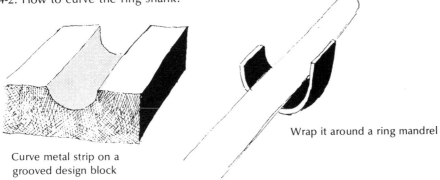

Curve metal strip on a
grooved design block

Wrap it around a ring mandrel

4-3. How to file top edge of the ornamental border.

4-4. Stretching a ring to desired size. First temper lightly, then pass it onto a ring mandrel. Stretch by tapping the ring to the line marking the desired size. If the desired size is larger than the largest size on the mandrel, you will have to cut the ring with a saw and add metal. Ordinarily, it is easy to stretch a ring from a half to a full size.

4-5. Add metal to enlarge a ring. Fit into place and solder.

MAKING AN OBLONG BROOCH

Described below are the steps you must follow to make the fish-shaped brooch shown. Begin by making a drawing of the fish, using a pencil or marker.

Procedure

1. Make the ornamental border for setting the stone that will be the fish's eye. (See section on making ornamental borders.)

2. Lightly temper 1.2 mm. thick square wire and, with a long-nose plier, shape it to the outline of the fish. Use a file to cut grooves where the metal must bend sharply. The point that forms the mouth should be narrowed with a file. Solder the completed outline of the fish to a 0.5 mm. thick sheet. Use 5% or 7% alloy solder. Trim around the outside with saw and file.

3. Flatten 0.8 mm. to 1 mm. round wire lightly with a roller. Temper and shape it to form the pattern inside the fish. Fit it into the fish and solder. To do this, put small amounts of solder in about 10 places. When this is done make the fins. Heat the end of 1.2 mm. round wire at the tip of a strong flame to make the silver balls (see directions on page 63). Make 16 balls. Set them along the length of the fish so they balance and solder to the back. To insure better contact, be sure to tap flat the part of the fin that will be soldered to the back of brooch.

4. Solder the eye of the fish in place.

5. Finally, solder on a clasp. Clean with acid. Check to make sure that solder is holding, then apply antiquing solution. As you can see in the photograph, the depressed areas of the brooch will be black while the raised ones will shine.

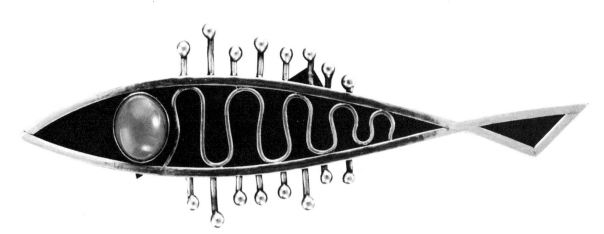

4-6. Oblong brooch. Silver with oxidized silver finish. The eye is a turquoise.

4-7. Step-by-step diagram for oblong brooch.

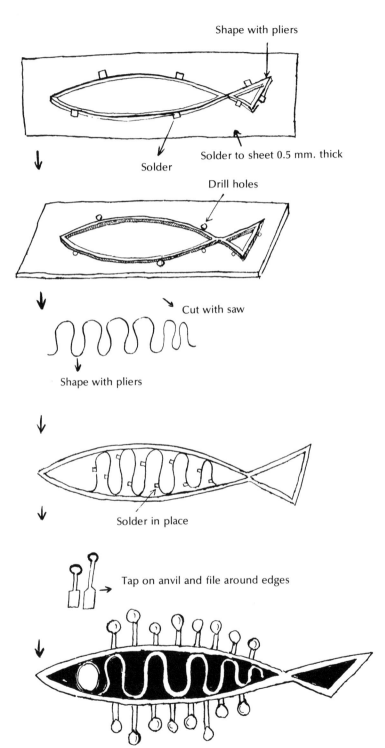

Shape with pliers

Solder to sheet 0.5 mm. thick

Solder

Drill holes

Cut with saw

Shape with pliers

Solder in place

Tap on anvil and file around edges

Solder on fins, eye, and clasp; finish with antiquing solution

MAKING PENDANTS

The ideas for the pendants shown in the photographs here came from ordinary things you might see every day. They are not difficult to make.

The pendant on this page is a crinkled smiling face. The spiral shaped eyes were suggested by long apple-skin peelings.

The fish pendant on the facing page at right has a stylish simplicity. Turquoise is used for the eyes. Similar pendants can be made with birds or butterflies as subjects.

The center pendant depicts a child's face and hands pressed against a window pane.

The pendant at left shows the skeleton of a fish on a platter, picked clean at dinner. Keep in mind that the everyday and the humorous can provide ideas for delightful pieces of jewelry.

4-8. Crinkled smiling face pendant.

Facing page

4-9. Three pendants — fish platter after dinner; child's face and hands pressed against a window pane; a pair of blue-eyed fish.

O Round holes are made with drill

◁ Triangles should be cut out

— Straight lines of bone structure
are cut with saw

4-10. Smiling face.

1. Make a sketch on paper, transfer it to metal sheet
0.8 mm. - 1 mm. thick. Cut out the outside border
and the eyes in a spiral fashion. Be careful not to cut
through the spirals.

2. From the same thickness of metal cut the nose
piece as shown in diagram. Solder in place. Drill a
hole and cut away mouth. Use pieces of melted
silver for eyelashes. Temper the eyes and push out
from face to give a three-dimensional feeling.

3. Apply antiquing solution, polish with metal
cleaner and burnisher.

4-11. Fish bones on platter. Sketch design and transfer to metal. Cut out with saw and trim with file.
Temper lightly, push out center of fish slightly.
Apply antiquing, polish with metal cleaner, attach
chain.

106

Add detail with
pointed graver

Cut out this part with saw

4-12. Hands and face pressed against window pane.

1. Draw sketch on paper and transfer to metal.
2. With narrow bit, drill holes at points where you will cut out the face, hands, and the pattern at bottom.
3. Cut shapes with saw and trim edges with a file. Use your saw carefully as this work is detailed. Solder on a loop for a chain.
4. Temper lightly and bend to add accent.
5. Apply antiquing and polish with metal cleaner. Attach chain.

4-13. A pair of blue-eyed fish.

1. Draw sketch on paper, transfer to metal, cut around with saw and file.
2. Cut out fishes, file inside edges.
3. With dapping ball press, make bowls to fit stones—
— turquoise were used in this pendant — and solder in place.
4. Use an antique finish or rhodium plate. Use cement to set the stone in bowl.

CHAINS AND CLASPS

Surprisingly, you often see fine pieces of jewelry hung on inferior chains. Since handcrafting chains is in fact time consuming, and they are, erroneously, considered by many as unimportant, chains have been neglected. This, in part, is the fault of designers who painstakingly handcraft a beautiful piece — then hang it on a readymade chain!

We should all keep in mind that chains are an integral part of design, and although making them requires a great deal of concentration it is most rewarding. If you take the time and the trouble, you can produce some really fine chains that exactly suit your tastes. Short or long, single or multiple, plain or ornate, no other item of jewelry is quite so adaptable for all seasons and occasions. Bracelets and belts fashioned of handmade chains can transform a simple dress into a costume.

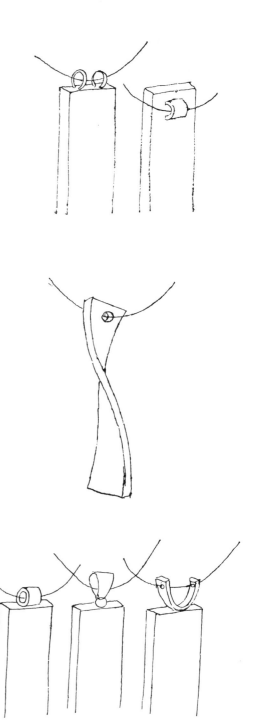

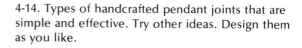

4-14. Types of handcrafted pendant joints that are simple and effective. Try other ideas. Design them as you like.

However, if you do decide to buy ready-made chains, buy interesting ones and add some original touches to overcome that mass-produced look.

The metal findings for necklaces, armlets, bracelets, earrings, brooches, tie clips, and cuff links may be purchased. Even when made of silver they are moderately priced.

The metal of the clasp should be strong enough to stand up under steady use. Your soldering job should be well done and checked frequently to see that it is holding. Where the findings of a piece are visible, they should be chosen with care as a component of your design.

A group of clasp designs simple enough for a beginner to attempt are described and illustrated on the next two pages.

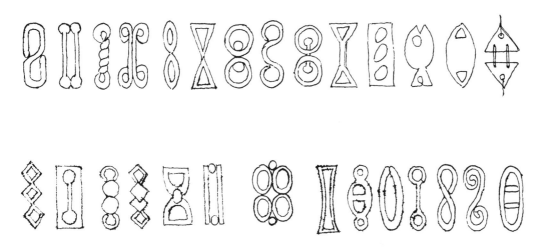

4-15. Ideas for handcrafted ornamental chain links. Make many from the same pattern and link to form a chain.

4-16. Step-by-step diagram for a snap clasp.

4-18. Step-by-step diagrams for a hinge clasp.

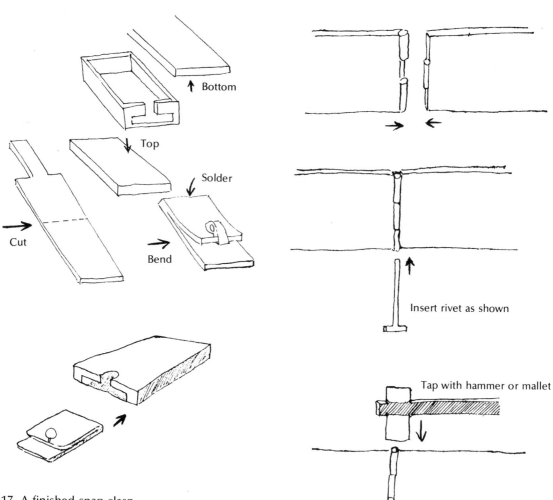

Bottom

Top

Solder

Cut

Bend

Insert rivet as shown

Tap with hammer or mallet

4-17. A finished snap clasp.

Clasp for necklace of many strands. Rivet holds strands in place.

Ends wrapped with thin leather strips.

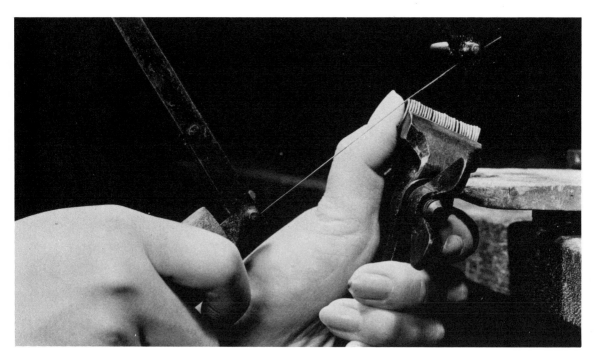

4-19. Making ring loops.

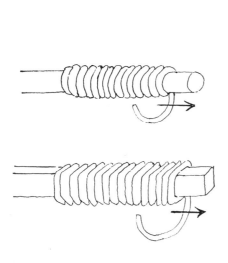

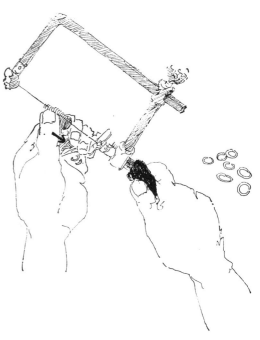

4-20. Wind tempered wire around a round or square rod and cut with saw.

4-21. Cut as shown. Hold loops in left hand, the saw in the right hand.

NECKLACE CONSTRUCTED ENTIRELY OF EIGHTEEN CARAT GOLD WIRE

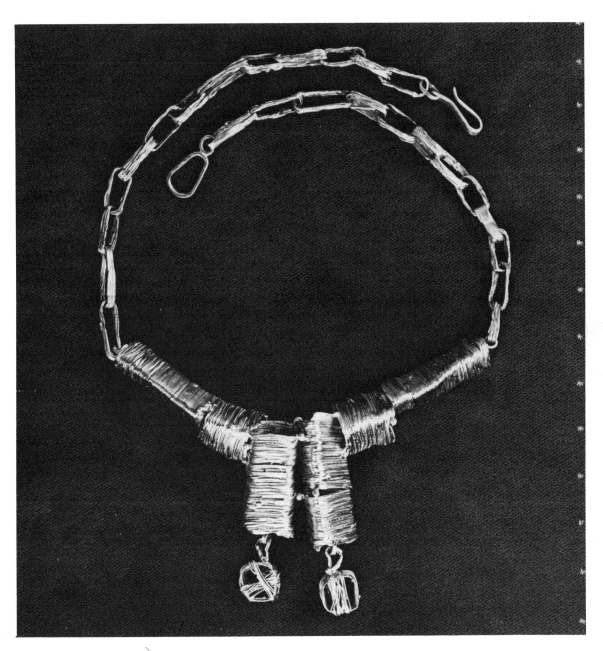

4-22. This beautiful and unusual necklace is not difficult to make. First prepare the various shapes out of cardboard or very stiff paper. Temper gold wire. Wind the tempered wire carefully around each shape. Burn out the cardboard base with your torch at very low flame. Solder. Link all the items. Solder joinings. Attach a handcrafted hook and ring clasp. See Color Plate I, page 2.

MAKING CUFF LINKS

The idea for these cuff links came from observing a pile of firewood stacked outside a farm house.

Procedure

1. Cut 12 pieces of 2 to 2.5 mm. round wire, each piece 17 mm. long, for each set of cuff links.

2. Solder the pieces into a pile, with three in the first layer, two in the middle and one as the top layer (see diagram). Use 5% or 7% alloy solder in pieces 1 mm. square. If too much solder is used the pieces will not fit together properly.

3. Prepare wrapping for the "firewood." Lightly temper about five lengths of 0.5 mm. round wire. Solder these onto a strip of 0.4 mm. thick sheet. The wire should be slightly larger than will be necessary to wrap around the pile of "firewood." Cut away the excess metal with a saw, then wrap around the "firewood" and solder at the bottom. Do not use too much solder or it will be difficult to finish the piece.

4. Solder clasp to the bottom of the pile. File the bottom so the clasp fits well. Insert rivet in the clasp. Now finish the surface. Possibilities for finishing include oxidizing the silver, or coating with gold or rhodium plate.

4-23. At right are cuff links made by soldering silver rods into the arrangement of a stack of firewood. Silver with rhodium finish. The striped ring at left is made with soldered square wire. Silver with oxidized silver finish. Diagrams for making this ring appear on page 116.

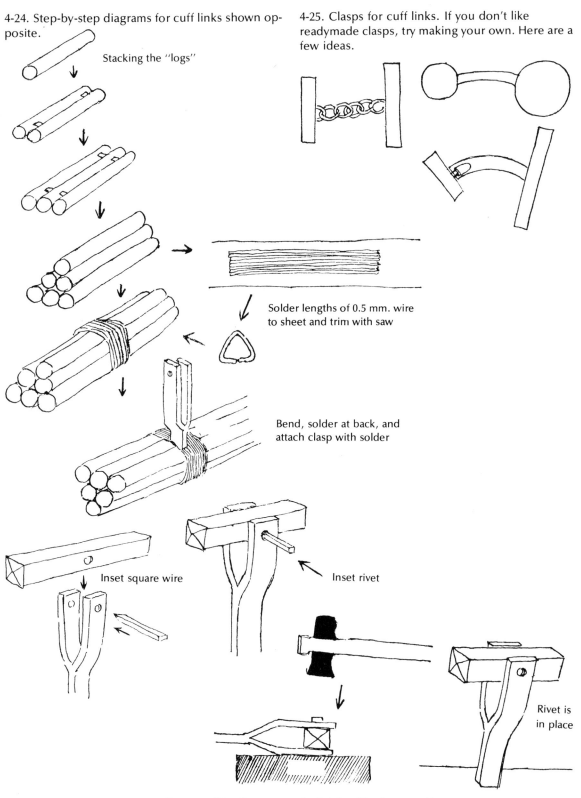

4-24. Step-by-step diagrams for cuff links shown opposite.

Stacking the "logs"

Solder lengths of 0.5 mm. wire to sheet and trim with saw

Bend, solder at back, and attach clasp with solder

4-25. Clasps for cuff links. If you don't like readymade clasps, try making your own. Here are a few ideas.

Inset square wire

Inset rivet

Rivet is in place

On an anvil tap the square wire lightly with a hammer. Do not tap too hard or the clasp will stick

MAKING A SOLDERED RING (2)

Procedure

1. Cut four lengths of 1 mm. square wire to the length needed for the size ring you wish to make, plus about ¾ inch more.

2. Solder wire to a 0.5 mm. thick sheet, leaving equal spaces between each piece. Apply small amounts of solder in several places.

3. Cut both ends with a saw. Bend to size on the ring mandrel. Cut to size. File. Solder ends together.

4. Work the surface with a fine file, the burnisher, and the scraper. Then give the ring an acid dip. Use the body of the burnisher rather than the tip.

5. Polish with a metal brush and apply antique finish. Clean the raised parts of the ring but leave the depressed areas black.

A photograph of this ring appears on page 114.

4-26. Step-by-step diagram for soldered ring.

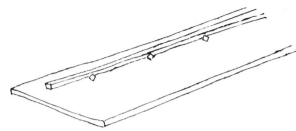

Solder 1 mm. square wire equal distances apart. In the diagram, the black stripes represent the square wire, not the antiqued depressions

Cut away excess sheet

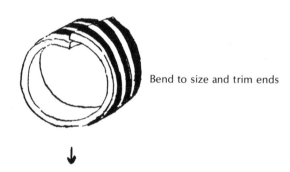

Bend to size and trim ends

Section to be soldered

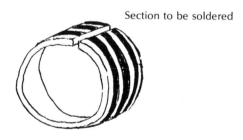

Completed ring. Polish and apply antiquing

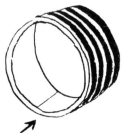

4-27. When a piece is finished, weigh it. Try feeling the weight in your hand or worn on your clothing. Remember, a piece that is too heavy is a failure. Heavy pieces made of gold, white gold, platinum, etc., will be expensive. Keep your pieces as light as possible.

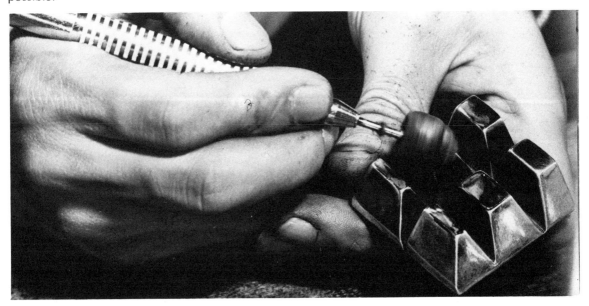

4-28. The photograph above shows finishing touches being put on a work with a flexible-shaft hand burnisher. This tool is not essential for the beginner. Polishing with metal cleaner gives good results.

MAKING A BUTTERFLY BROOCH

The butterfly brooch pictured here (enlarged) has an oxidized silver finish. It has double-layered wings to express a sensation of flight. Any kind of stone may be used, but an uncut cabochon shape is best. Study the diagrams opposite.

Procedure

1. First make ornamental borders for the stones. They are variations of the borders described earlier (page 100). Make wire twists to fit the stones and press them down lightly with a roller. (Setting the stones will be the last step.) Solder pieces of 0.5 mm. sheet silver to the bottoms of the borders, trim around the outside, then cut out the center, leaving an inside rim about 2 mm. to 3 mm. wide.

2. Make four wings. Use 0.6 mm. to 0.8 mm. sheet silver. The wing patterns shown at bottom right in the diagram are actual size and may be used as a guide. Cut out with a saw. Solder the ornamental borders in place, and then cut away wing metal under the centers of the ornamental border, leaving a narrow band, about 2 mm. This is especially important if you are using a transparent stone requiring light from below. The stone will be set later with cement.

3. To make the body, cut an appropriate strip of 0.5 mm. thick sheet, groove it with a file, temper lightly, and bend to make an oblong box open on two sides as shown in the diagram. Be sure to leave a space between the ends. This box will be the underside of the body, and it must be left open because it provides a runoff for the acid and water that will seep in while you are soldering. Solder 0.5 mm. sheets to sides and trim away excess with saw and file.

4. When the body is complete, prepare some fairly large silver balls and solder in place as eyes.

5. Now solder the wings to the body. Attach both lower wings first, then the upper ones. Put asbestos between the upper and lower wings before soldering, to keep them in their proper positions. Check the soldering job and give the piece an acid dip. Turn the brooch over and solder on the clasp, slightly above center. Use a quick flowing 9% alloy solder. Finish with an antiquing solution and polish with metal cleaner and burnisher. Finally, set the stones in place with epoxy or cement.

See this brooch photographed in full color on Plate VI, page 11.

4-29. Butterfly brooch.

4-30. Step-by-step diagrams for making butterfly brooch.

Fit the wire twists to the stones

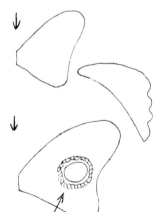

Solder ornamental borders into their proper positions on the wings

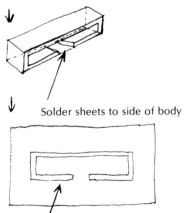

Solder sheets to side of body

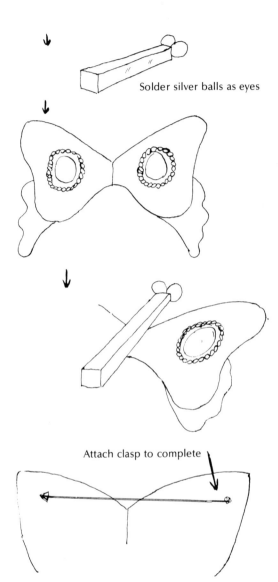

Solder silver balls as eyes

Attach clasp to complete

Pattern for the wings in actual size

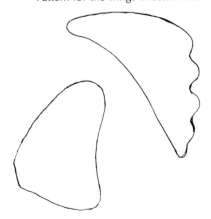

5.

SYMBOLISM OF RINGS IN HISTORY

Rings have played a surprising number of roles over the ages and many legends have grown up about them. In ancient times the Egyptians used rings as money: many rings of various sizes and value were slipped on a large ring to be used as currency — a forerunner of our wallet and change purse.

Rings also came into use as impression seals; this type is the ancestor of the signet ring worn today. Originally, seal rings were a variation of the cylindrical seal and were worn on a chain around neck or arm. As time went by they came to be regarded as personal adornments and were eventually worn as finger ornaments. The prized beetle-shaped seal rings called scarabs originated in Egypt, and authentic ancient Egyptian scarab rings are considered valuable antiques.

As is still the case, important dealings required the mark or seal of a responsible person; whoever was given the seal ring of such a person could wield the power held by the owner (forerunner of our power of attorney?). The custom developed of placing one's seal ring on the finger of the person one married. This represented absolute trust on the part of the spouse, and acceptance of the ring symbolized that the spouse was in honor bound not to betray the trust so placed. This custom of exchanging rings began in Egypt, was passed down to the Greeks and Romans, and is still in practice today (our double-ring marriage ceremony).

According to ancient Egyptian records, these rings were placed on the third finger of the left

5-1. Money rings. 5-2. Seal ring.

hand, believed to be directly connected to the heart. Thus the ring, given as a symbol of love, was placed on a spot connected with the heart, which was also symbolic of love. It was believed that wedding rings on the third finger of the left hand were kept pure by the warm clean blood flowing directly from the heart.

Another reason for choosing the left hand was that it was regarded as representative of obedience and trust while the right hand symbolized power and authority. The third finger may also have been chosen because it is the finger most limited in movement and therefore in use, thus the least likely to be hurt.

An amusing story about the ring finger comes to us from ancient England. During a wedding ceremony, at the words "In the name of the Father," the ring was placed on the bride's *thumb*. At the words "In the name of the Son," the ring was removed and placed on her *index finger*. And at the words "In the name of the Holy Ghost," it was removed again and placed on the *middle finger*. When the "Amen" was said, ending the prayer, the ring was placed on the *ring finger*, where it remained.

RINGS IN ANCIENT GREECE

Rings were introduced into Greece from the Eastern countries. Greeks began wearing rings on the ring finger of the left hand but later came to wear them on the index finger and the little finger. Although Grecian rings were primarily made of gold, semiprecious metals were also employed. Jasper, quartz, ruby, and chalcedony were used as stones.

As the Egyptians did before them, the Greeks made use of seal rings, but those of the Greeks were much smaller in size. Two methods were used in carving. The design could be lowered (intaglio), in which case agate and chalcedony were used, or the design could be raised (carved), in which case ruby, quartz, and jasper were used.

Imitation gems first appeared in ancient Greece. During the Hellenic period, as interest in rings grew, dishonest merchants took advantage of their customers and palmed off artificial gems as real. The exact method used for making these gems is not known but apparently they applied color to the backs of less valuable transparent gems. Though the method was crude, when done by a skilled craftsman it was effective in deceiving gullible buyers.

The custom of wearing rings to ensure magical powers or ward off evil spirits has its roots in ancient Greece, and was also popular during the Middle Ages.

According to Greek mythology, it was the god Hermes who gave human beings rings that could perform miracles. Among the magical rings of the Greeks were those that made one invisible, that produced wealth and good fortune, guaranteed love, and protected health.

RINGS OF THE ANCIENT ROMANS

Most early Roman rings were made of iron. Gold was used much later. The Romans also produced some remarkable silver rings wound into circular designs and spiral shell patterns.

Iron was used even for wedding rings. Iron is a hard metal and people seemed to feel that rings made of it symbolized a lasting, unchanging bond between man and wife. Sometimes natural magnets were selected as stones for wedding rings to further symbolize the strong attraction between two people.

Thumb rings were also popular. They had no special significance but suggested distinction, wealth, and character.

Portrait rings were in favor at this time. An image of a god, revered as one's ancestor, or an honored living person would be carved into this type of ring. The ring worn by Caesar bore the likeness of the goddess Aphrodite, who was considered his ancestress.

Another unusual ring was one worn over the first joint of the finger. These rings, lavishly ornamented, were worn as emblems by the rich, proud of their wealth and power. By wearing them on the first joint, the imperious Romans could display them to advantage constantly.

The Romans produced still another remarkable ring called a key ring. These rings were worn originally by the wives of Romans as a badge of their authority in the household and their absolute power in kitchen and wine cellar. Although established and worn as a status symbol, the key you see attached to the ring was a real key that worked — perhaps it opened the wine cellar.

The greatest oddity among ancient Roman rings was the poison ring, and it was still in use during the sixteenth and seventeenth centuries. As most of us know, these rings concealed a dose of poison. They were first designed for use in case one was taken as prisoner. In those times, death by one's own hand often seemed preferable to the humiliation and probable torture of captivity. Later, the poison ring became an underhand weapon for use against a personal or political enemy.

During the Middle Ages church rings, which were bestowed on the clergy, made their appearance; their role was similar to that played by the rings worn by royalty. They were used to signify the dignity and authority of churchmen, denoting their position in the church, as well as symbolizing the spiritual unity of the church. The Pope, the cardinals, the bishops, and the abbots all wore special rings.

Although most rings of this period served as seal rings, the craftsmen's skill at creating purely ornamental rings was striking. Rings carved with portraits of their owners were popular, and were widely used as engagement rings and wedding rings, and for gifts.

Magical rings reappeared. Believed to endow their owners with magical and supernatural powers, these rings were used by all classes of people. Here are two examples: it was believed that if one rotated the stone of a certain ring, one would become invisible, while the simple wearing of another would enable one to converse with birds. It was also believed that the stones, bone, and metal used in rings had in themselves strange powers. The tooth of a wolf gave its wearer unimaginably terrible powers to resist an enemy's attack. Badger's teeth were valued for bringing wealth and good fortune. Some magical rings were said to have the power to change the colors of things, and could be used to detect the presence of poison in food or drink.

It was thought that certain inscriptions carved on rings might conceal mysterious and superhuman powers, and one such ring was said to have special curative effects on epilepsy and convulsions.

Religious rings for laymen were typical of this period. Made of gold, bronze, ivory, and other handsome materials, they often included a prayer to the Virgin Mary, and were sometimes adorned with a globe from which a crucifix projected.

5-3. Royal Roman thumb ring.

5-4. First joint finger ring.

5-5. Key ring.

5-6. Poison ring.

RINGS DURING THE RENAISSANCE

Throughout the sixteenth and seventeenth centuries rings mostly represented love and affection. Men and women of these times were not content to simply wear their rings only on their fingers — they also strung them on chains, which they wore as necklaces, taking great pride in the possession of many rings. Rings worn in this way can be seen in period portraits.

Bouquet rings, completely circled with a flower pattern had much appeal. Words in praise of love were often carved inside.

Another type of unusual ring was also indicative of the century's deep involvement in the love relationship between people. Such rings were often set with gems whose initial letters spelled out either a wish connected with a lover, or the name of the loved one. This is an example:

L   apis lazuli
O   pal
V   erd antique
E   merald

M   alachite
E   merald

S   apphire
A   methyst
R   uby
A   methyst
D   iamond
O   pal

Reading down, the initial letters of the gem names give us, "Love me Sarado." Sarado may have been the name of a lover, or the message may be, "Love me Sara do." Today's practice of inscribing the initials of a couple inside of their wedding rings may have had its origin in this custom.

THE STORY OF THE ESSEX RING

There is the famous tale involving Queen Elizabeth I and a ring. The Queen presented the Earl of Essex with a favorite royal ring, saying that should anything happen to him that required her aid, he should send the ring back to her and his request would be granted.

Essex was unjustly imprisoned for the crime of high treason and sentenced to death. In his despair, he sent the ring to the Queen with a note pleading that his life be spared. Unfortunately, both the ring and the note fell into the hands of the wife of Essex's arch rival. Since the ring was so beautiful and she was so ambitious, she decided to destroy the note and keep the ring. Waiting in vain for his Queen to grant his request, Essex went to his death on the executioner's block.

Later, the betrayer became mortally ill. Fearing she would not live even one more day, she confessed her crime to the Queen. In a frenzy of grief and anger, tormented by thoughts that Essex had died hating her for dishonoring her vow, Elizabeth attacked the dying woman. The Queen's own death soon afterwards was said to be due in part to anguish over her unfulfilled vow to Essex.

5-7. Queen Elizabeth I.

ACKNOWLEDGMENTS

I wish to extend my thanks to those who gave me help and encouragement in the preparation of this book: first to Mr. Ken Domon, whose photographs and support were so important to this work; to Mr. Ushio Kido and Mr. Tsutsumi Katsuo who took additional photographs; to Malcolm Varon, who designed and did the photography for the front and back jacket of this edition; to Mr. Mukasa Noboru who did the diagrams and drawings; and finally to Kawabe Takehiko, Fukuchi Yochihiko, and Nakahara Ryukichi for their editorial assistance.

Takashi Wada

LIST OF USEFUL BOOKS

all prices subject to change

IDEAS FOR JEWELRY. Ian Davidson. New York: Watson-Guptill Publications, Inc., 1972. $7.95

INVENTIVE JEWELRY-MAKING. Ramona Solberg. New York: Van Nostrand Reinhold, 1972. $8.95

JEWELRY-MAKING FOR BEGINNERS. Edward J. Soukup. Mentone, Calif.: Gembooks, 1973. Paperback. $2.00

JEWELRY: FORM & TECHNIQUE. Michael D. Grando. New York: Van Nostrand Reinhold, 1970. $5.95

JEWELRY-MAKER'S HANDBOOK. Iva L. Geisinger. Mentone, Calif.: Gembooks, 1973. Paperback. $2.00

JEWELRY-MAKING AS A HOBBY: *An illustrated guide for beginners.* Robert Wald. New York: Association Press, 1973. Paperback. $5.95

JEWELRY: QUEEN OF CRAFTS. William. R. Sanford. Riverside, N.J.: Macmillan Publishing Company, Inc., 1970. $8.95

MAKING JEWELRY BY THE LOST WAX PROCESS. Greta Pack. New York: Van Nostrand Reinhold, 1968. $6.95

MAKE·YOUR OWN ELEGANT JEWELRY. R. Boulay. New York: Sterling Publishing Company, Inc., 1972. Little Craft Book. $2.95

MODERN JEWELRY AND TECHNIQUE. Irena Brynner. New York: Van Nostrand Reinhold, 1968. $7.95

TREASURY OF JEWELS AND GEMS. Mona Curran. Buchanan, N.Y.: Emerson Books, Inc., 1962. $5.95

VAN NOSTRAND STANDARD CATALOG OF GEMS. John Sinkankas. New York: Van Nostrand Reinhold, 1968. $8.95

THE WORLD OF JEWEL STONES. Michael Weinstein. Yonkers, N.Y.: Sheridan House, Inc., 1958. $20.00

SUPPLIERS

If not available in your locality, equipment, tools, findings, metals, stones, and other supplies can be obtained from the firms listed below. All issue catalogs and fill mail orders.

ALLCRAFT, 22 West 48th Street
New York, N.Y. 10036
Tel: (212) 246–4740

AMPEX CASTING CORP., 71 Fifth Avenue,
New York, N.Y. 10016
Tel: (212) 581-1141

GAMZON BROS., INC., 21 West 46th Street,
New York, N.Y. 10036
Tel: (212) 581-2550

T.B. HAGSTOZ & SON, 709 Sansom Street,
Philadelphia, Pa. 19106
Tel: (215) Wa 2-1627 — 1628

INTERNATIONAL GEM CORPORATION, 15 Maiden
Lane, New York, N.Y. 10013
Tel: (212) Co 7-8900

I. SHOR COMPANY, 71 Fifth Avenue,
New York, N.Y. 10016
Tel: (212) Wa 4-2200

MYRON TOBACK, INC., 27 West 47th Street,
New York, N.Y. 10036
Tel: (212) 247-4750

INDEX